Salt Water Game Fishing

Also from Westphalia Press

westphaliapress.org

The Idea of the Digital University

Bulwarks Against Poverty in America

Treasures of London

Avate Garde Politician

L'Enfant and the Freemasons

Baronial Bedrooms

Making Trouble for Muslims

Philippine Masonic Directory ~ 1918

Paddle Your Own Canoe

Opportunity and Horatio Alger

Careers in the Face of Challenge

Bookplates of the Kings

Hymns to the Gods

Freemasonry in Old Buffalo

Original Cables from the Pearl Harbor Attack

Social Satire and the Modern Novel

The Essence of Harvard

The Genius of Freemasonry

A Definitive Commentary on Bookplates

James Martineau and Rebuilding Theology

Bohemian San Francisco

The Wizard

Crime 3.0

Anti-Masonry and the Murder of Morgan

Understanding Art

Spies I Knew

Lodge "Himalayan Brotherhood" No. 459 C.E.

Ancient Masonic Mysteries

Collecting Old Books

Masonic Secret Signs and Passwords

Death Valley in '49

Lariats and Lassos

Mr. Garfield of Ohio

The Wisdom of Thomas Starr King

The French Foreign Legion

War in Syria

Naturism Comes to the United States

New Sources on Women and Freemasonry

Designing, Adapting, Strategizing in Online Education

Gunboat and Gun-runner

Memoirs of a Poor Relation

Espionage!

Bohemian San Francisco

Tales of Old Japan

Salt Water Game Fishing

by Charles Frederick Holder

WESTPHALIA PRESS
An imprint of Policy Studies Organization

Salt Water Game Fishing

Westphalia Press
An imprint of Policy Studies Organization
1527 New Hampshire Ave., NW
Washington, D.C. 20036
info@ipsonet.org

ISBN-13: 978-1-63391-232-8
ISBN-10: 1633912329

Cover design by Taillefer Long at Illuminated Stories:
www.illuminatedstories.com

Daniel Gutierrez-Sandoval, Executive Director
PSO and Westphalia Press

Updated material and comments on this edition
can be found at the Westphalia Press website:
www.westphaliapress.org

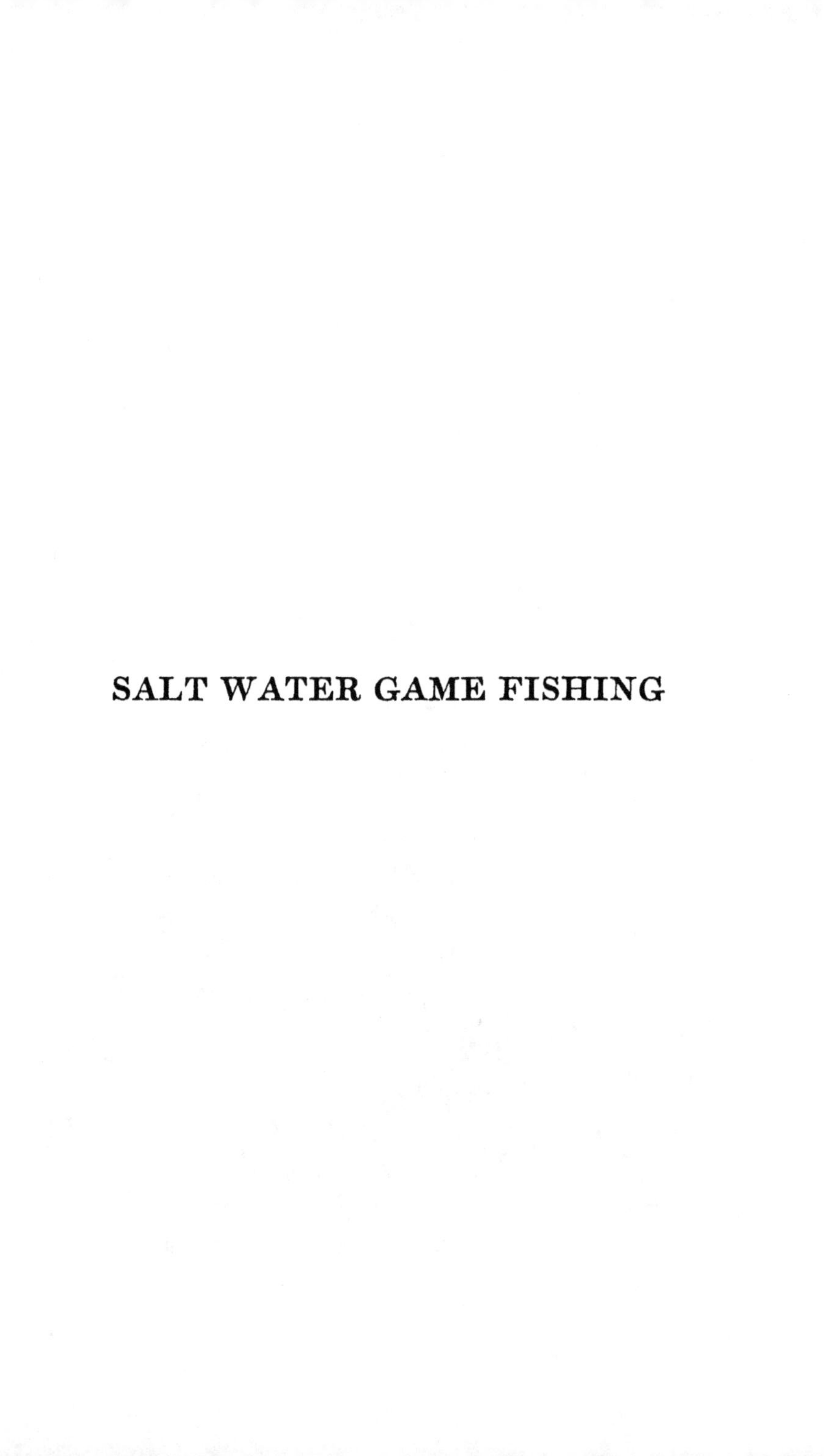

SALT WATER GAME FISHING

Author in a Santa Catalina fishing launch

SALT WATER GAME FISHING

BY

CHARLES FREDERICK HOLDER

Author of "Big Game at Sea," etc.

PREFACE

IN the present volume of this series I have attempted to give the angler interested in sea angling alone some general idea of the marine fishes of the United States to which the term game may legitimately be applied. The subject at best is an exhaustless one, and it is somewhat difficult to condense to the essentials and compress it into a little volume which the sea angler can slip into his pocket. I am aware, then, that my sense of proportion may be at fault and that I may have eliminated or omitted some of the very points the reader may desire, but I have endeavored to put myself in his place and have given only the essentials.

As an illustration, a large volume could be written on tackle alone. A ponderous book would be required to describe fully the fishing grounds around New York, Fire Island, etc. This is also true of Florida or California, so I have only hinted at the details and fishes to be found in certain localities.

For the convenience of the angler I have divided the fields of angling into geographical areas, and have given the fishes, the bait used, the tackle to be employed, so that the angler can go to the region knowing what to expect and what to take, and arriving, can obtain the lesser details from boatmen. I have fished nearly all the seaboards from Maine to Aransas Pass, Texas, and from the Gulf of California to Oregon on the Pacific slope, and have taken, I think, all the fishes described or mentioned in the volume. Two regions stand out in strong relief—that of Florida and the Southern California islands. In the former the region one hundred and fifty miles north or south of Cape Sable is the greatest tropical sea angling ground in the world, as here the angler floats over coral reefs and catches the purely *tropical* game: jacks, kingfish, tarpon, and snappers, yet is but a few hours from New York. There is no place just like it, as a fishing region does not depend on its fishes alone, but must have comforts for your modern angler. I fished the Florida reef in 1860, before there was even a telegraph wire from Key West to the coast. To-day you can go to Key West by rail; the finest hotels in the world line the east and west coast, and the day will come when Key West, with its incomparable winter climate and sport, will be a favorite for anglers and tourists.

Equal to this, yet totally different, is the angling region of Southern California islands—Santa Catalina and San Clemente, twenty or more miles from Los Angeles, a city of nearly two-thirds of a million people. Here the catch is *semi-tropic*—the leaping tuna, the yellow-fin tuna, the long-fin tuna, the white sea bass, and, most important, the leaping swordfish, which attracts to this region the anglers of the world. Here the Tuna Club has taken form, including some of the most influential and distinguished men in America and England, who have conserved the fisheries and elevated the standards of sport. England has the lead in angling clubs, due to its age and maturity, but America is forging to the front, and scores of influential clubs like the Santa Catalina Island Tuna Club, the Aransas Pass Tarpon Club, the Asbury Park Fishing Club, the Southern California Rod and Reel Club of Los Angeles, are coming to the fore; not alone to catch fish, but to establish standards of sport, conserve the fisheries, and aid in the establishment of game laws and see that they are observed. Upon the intelligent angler depends the fish supply of the future, as they stand for protection, and without their intervention the alien market fishermen would make desolate the seas, rivers, lakes, and streams in less than a decade. The sea angler of to-day is not only an angler, he is a conservator of the people's interest.

C. F. H.

Pasadena, Cal.

CONTENTS

CONTENTS

ILLUSTRATIONS

CHAPTER I

THE GROUNDS

FOR the convenience of the reader, the angling grounds for sea game fish in America may be divided into several great divisions. They are so located that the sportsman can begin at a definite point and swing around an angling circle, covering the entire field in a satisfactory manner and during the trip traverse the most interesting portions of America. They are as follows:

New England

First. The New England fishing ground, including the New England States and the vicinity of Cape Cod, Block Island, etc. Here we have the bluefish, the swordfish (*Xiphias*), the striped bass, halibut, the pollock, blackfish, and mackerel, distinctively game fishes, and many more, such as tautog, cod, hake, haddock, all found in water of greater or less depth, not always game, but valuable; and numbers of small fry, as the cunner, flounder, sculpin, and others, interesting at times with rod and light lines.

This region, besides the coast from " 'way down East," should embrace the mouth of the St. Lawrence River, Nova Scotia, and New Brunswick (for the tuna fishing), down alongshore to Block Island, where there is excellent sport with the bluefish, and at times tuna, while the big swordfish also waits.

Various steamers from Boston reach Nova Scotia. The mouth of the St. Lawrence and Prince Edward's Island are available from Montreal, Quebec, and Boston, the trip being easy and interesting. The coast of Maine near Booth Bay, Squirrel Island, and Ocean Point abounds in excellent fishing from the rocks, though it is not over exciting. At Ogunquit I have had excellent sport for pollock with a fly and trout rod. From here I went out to the vicinity of Boon Island, ten miles offshore, for halibut, cod, tuna, swordfish, sharks (dogfish), the latter and cod predominating. Not far from here some years ago one hundred tunas were taken, each of which weighed over one thousand pounds. They were caught in a net in Gloucester harbor.

All alongshore there are fishes of some sort,

from the dainty cunner I caught when a boy at Red Rock, Lynn, Nahant or Swamscott, to the larger fry off Egg Rock. Excellent fishing is found down by Buzzard's Bay. From New Bedford a steamer may be taken to Nantucket, where most invigorating bluefish trolling may be had and a variety of game, including big sharks not found inshore.

On the strangely named islands off New Bedford, as Cuttyhunk, there are still some striped bass, but not to compare with the sport thirty or forty years ago, when many clubs made these islands famous. Block Island is within easy reach of New Bedford, Providence, and Newport, and may be termed the headquarters of the bluefish and the swordfish industry.

The Tuna Club of Santa Catalina Island set a new pace for anglers in taking a 355-pound swordfish, the feat being accomplished by Mr. Boschen of New York. This was the first Mediterranean, or what is known as the Atlantic, swordfish (*Xiphias*) ever taken with rod and reel, although Dr. Gifford Pinchot played one four hours in 1910. It is particularly interesting that this fish should have been taken at Santa Catalina. Why this has not become a sport in the Block Island region long before lies in the fact that to take the fish in the Atlantic one must go to the open and rough water, while at Santa Catalina the game is played in the lee of the great islands, though twenty or more miles at sea and often in water as calm as a lake, an essential when the game is large and menacing.

Fisher's Island, in Long Island Sound, is reached from New London by steamer, and some of the best bluefish, blackfish, and bass fishing I have ever had has been about this island. I often went out and landed my bluefish in the blue, swift-running currents, and half an hour later had the game served for breakfast in the little inn—a dish for the gods, and no one knows the real bluefish unless he has had this experience of immediate eating. With the pollock this rule is even more imperative; it should be eaten at once when taken from the water.

New York and New Jersey

Second. The New York and New Jersey region. This includes the blackfish, the bass, the tunny, weakfish, drum, striped bass, bluefish, mackerel, channel bass, sea bass and many smaller fishes. New York ranks next to London in its interest in angling.

Every wharf has its devotees, and special steamers run out to the banks, loaded with anglers, during the summer, and the pastime has its own patrons, its deep-sea tackle, its rods, reels and lines. Then there are numerous places down the harbor where the weakfish and the drumfish are taken from boats. In the bay near Coney Island I have watched the hauling of a fyke-net and noted the extraordinary variety of fishes caught prowling about the shallows at night, ranging from an occasional tarpon to the channel bass and striped bass, with sharks, rays, and goosefish.

The various inlets on the outer coast of Long Island afford good fishing, easy of access from New York by various lines. The cream of the fishing of this region is that which has the Asbury Park, N. J., Fishing Club as a center of radiation. The fine channel bass or spot comes into the surf to feed and the angler fishes standing on the beach or in the waves. Asbury Park is within a short distance of New York. An important center for striped bass is Harvey Cedars. Following down the coast we come to the great Chesapeake Bay, which abounds in fine fish, as the triple-tail. From here on a change is evident, although some of the Florida fishes, as the tarpon, migrate north, perhaps in the Gulf Stream. To reach the bay, steamers can be taken at Baltimore, or there are boats which leave New York direct for Norfolk. At Old Point and towns on the east shore, boatmen or professionals can be found who will take the angler out.

FLORIDA

Third. The Florida region, which extends from Virginia to Cuba, includes the tarpon, amberjack, sheepshead, barracuda, ladyfish, bonefish, jacks, snappers, kingfish, cero, sailfish, parrot-fish, and an endless variety of small fry, from the angel- and parrot-fishes to the grunts and porgies.

The angler who proposes to make the Florida trip can now reach Key West in a Pullman car in practically two days; if in winter he can almost go to sleep in a winter land and awaken in summer. This is due to modern facilities and the new Flagler railway, which extends out over the reef to Key West, opening up one of the greatest angling regions of the world—that of the Florida reef.

Good fishing is found all along the coast of Florida and Georgia, especially at the mouth of the St. Mary and St. John rivers, and all down the Indian River country, where there is a chain of beautiful hotels, from St. Augustine, Miami, and around the Cape, up the inside of the Gulf to Tampa; the entire region forming a real angler's paradise. An angler's camp or headquarters has been established at Long Key, where launches, rowboats, and sailboats can be obtained for the outside big game fishing.

The Gulf

Fourth. There is a peculiar fascination about these islands, at least to me, as I knew them well years ago, when they were a *terra incognita* to the world and only reached by boat from St. Augustine or from Key West by sponger. Now steamers run up and down the coast from Tampa to Key West and Cuba, or from New York to Key West. So, too, with Galveston. Steamers connect it with New York, and it is a short and agreeable trip in the cars *via* the Southern Pacific or Sunset route. Here is the Galveston Tarpon Club and an extraordinary breakwater or jetty that extends out into the Gulf affording fine sport to the most exacting angler.

About one hundred miles south of Galveston, on a big inland sea like the Indian River, is Port Aransas, where the Tarpon Club holds forth. This is reached by rail from San Antonio, Texas, and is, all things considered, one of the best sea angling points for tarpon on the Gulf. It is comfortable, on the water, and not too hot ashore in August. Tampico can be included in this region from an angling standpoint, and can be reached by rail from the interior and by boat from New York and possibly New Orleans.

The Pacific Coast

Fifth. The Pacific coast can be divided into two distinct fields of sea angling: one from Alaska and Vancouver to about San Francisco; the other from Monterey to San Diego. In the north the sea angling is mainly the salmon, which is taken trolling at Vancouver with a spoon; sea-trout at Eureka; halibut, rock cod, striped bass, salmon, etc., in San Francisco Bay; while at Capitola, Santa Cruz, and Carmel there is excellent trolling for salmon in July, August, and September. Good and often palatial hotels are found, and the angler, particularly at Del Monte, where there is a salmon cannery, finds all the facilities for angling for the great Chinook salmon.

Going south into the last field, angling is to be had at various points, as San Luis Obispo, where there is excellent sport with white sea bass—a giant weakfish, and all alongshore in season the steelhead is in evidence. At the Santa Barbara Islands we shall meet the bonito and albacore in numbers, and when we arrive at Santa Catalina and the U. S. Government island—San Clemente, one hundred miles south, we are in the heart of a wonderful sea angling country, justly famous all over the world. This is due to the abundance of large game fishes on their spawning-beds, which Dr. Jordan states are about the islands, and the fact that Santa Catalina, twenty-two miles in length, lies so that it constitutes a lee and smooth, lake-like water twenty or thirty miles out in the Pacific. This permits the use of light tackle, and together with the fact that the region three miles from shore cannot be netted in the future, gives the angler the promise of the best sport.

The great current, Kuro Shiwo, the Black Current of Japan, sweeps across the North Pacific and down the coast, and to this, doubtless, is due the presence at Santa Catalina and

San Clemente of many semi-tropic fishes or fishes common to Japan. The swordfish, taken here in large numbers with rod and reel, is so common in Japan that it has a Japanese name, *Tetrapturus mitsukuii.*

The game fishes found here are the leaping tuna, two swordfishes—*Xiphias* and *Tetrapturus*—the yellow-fin tuna, the long-fin tuna, two bonitos, the barracuda, sheepshead, rock bass of many varieties, the black sea bass, white sea bass, sea-trout, roncador, halibut, surf-fish, bony fish, and many more.

The best fishing has been at Santa Catalina, San Clemente, and the Coronado Islands, one hundred miles to the south; but the latter are barren rocks, in Mexican waters, while Santa Catalina has two fully equipped towns, Avalon and Cabrillo and a summer population of ten thousand or more.

One can reach this region from London or Paris in two weeks; from New York in five days. Los Angeles, a modern city of 600,000 inhabitants, is the central point, having various lines of railroads, and there are various lines of steamers to it through the Panama Canal from the great ports of the world. Arriving in Los Angeles, the angler rides to the port in half or three-quaterrs of an hour, there taking the steamer *Cabrillo* or *Hermosa* to Santa Catalina. If the destination is San Clemente Island, twenty miles further out, a launch must be chartered, as there is often a heavy sea going or coming. This can be avoided by making the trip early in the morning, leaving either island by four or five A. M., the voyage requiring about three and a half hours.

In a general way these fields of angling activity include all the sea angling in America. But we have Hawaii and the Philippines, and Bermuda and the Windward Islands are near at hand. In the Florida reef and the two islands—Santa Catalina and San Clemente—we have the best sea angling grounds in the world.

CHAPTER II

TACKLE SUGGESTIONS

MR. SAMUEL G. CAMP in his "Fishing Kits and Equipment"* has so thoroughly exhausted the subject of tackle that I can not do better than to recommend the book to the angler, and also refer briefly to the specific tackle used in the various sea angling fields indicated in the following pages.

A revolution has taken place among the sea anglers of the world, and to-day fishes are taken on tackle so light as to have been considered impossible fifteen years ago. This reformation was brought about by the Santa Catalina Island Tuna Club. In 1886 I took a black bass rod with a light trout line to Santa Catalina. It was the first ever seen in these dulcet waters. At that time, or soon after, it was the custom to go out with big hand-lines and

* OUTING *Handbook No. 7.*

Sea angling rods used by the Author

catch half a ton of splendid yellowtails, a fish that resembles a salmon and tips the scales at from twenty to fifty pounds.

It was to regulate this sport, establish a high standard, that I established this club, which has become famous the world over. The club has given tournaments to encourage the use of light tackle, and its influence has so spread over the world that nearly everywhere light rods and fine lines are now used. With such tackle I landed a 183-pound tuna. I killed a 95-pounder with a twelve-ounce yellowtail rod and a No. 18 line. I took a 17-pounder on an eight-ounce ten-foot Divine-made trout rod and an E enameled line. Others, among them Mr. T. McD. Potter, Col. John E. Stearns, Dr. Gifford Pinchot, Mr. J. E. Coxe, Mr. Boschen, and Mr. Arthur J. Eddy, took fishes of large size with No. 21, No. 18 and No. 6 lines and so revolutionized the sport.

The Tuna Club collaborated with a number of clubs in America, France, and England to make this universal, and so the tackle reform went around the world, and to-day the anglers of the Tuna Club all over the country have had the satisfaction of securing from the legislature a law recognizing Santa Catalina, or its shore and three miles off, as a spawning-ground; a movement not in the interest of the angler alone, but the consumer, as the market-men were, as is always the case, overdoing the netting and fast driving off the big market fish, particularly the leaping tuna, which was, before the netting, the great game fish here, but now is rare. It is expected that the non-netting law will bring them back.*

All the angling done in Southern California waters is of this light tackle persuasion, and it has resulted in much new business for the great houses, as the rods demanded are the finest split bamboo, greenheart and noibwood (or hickory), and of a light, small size.

The Tuna Club advocates for the tuna and fish of over one hundred pounds a rod not over sixteen ounces in weight; the tip not less than six feet. The line permitted is of twenty-four strands, which has a breaking strength of two pounds to the strand; hence such a line will lift a dead weight of forty-eight pounds. This is seldom used. I took my 183-pound tuna with a twenty-one-thread line, the breaking strength forty-two pounds. With this tackle the late Col. C. P. Morehous took a

* The season of 1913, two months after the law went into effect, saw the finest yellow-fin tuna angling in ten years.

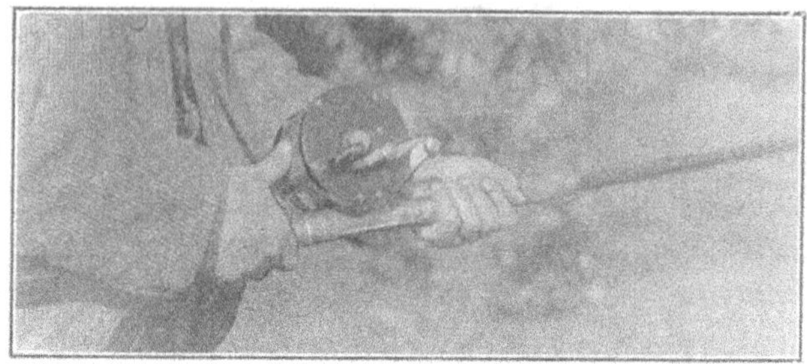

Right view of reel in readiness, right thumb resting on the leather brake, left hand grasping upper cork grip.

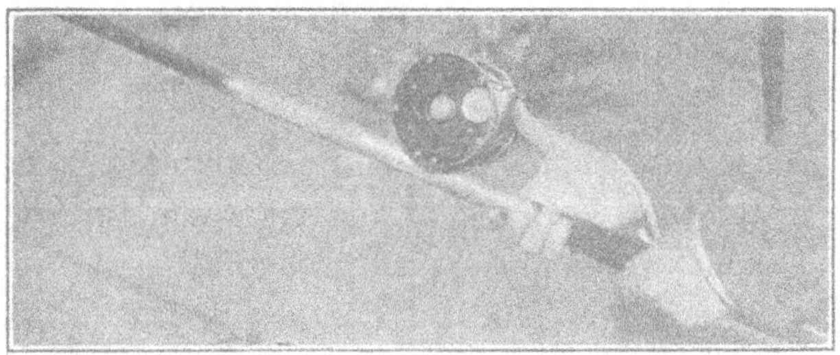

Tuna or Tarpon reel showing position of the thumb pressing the leather brake.

Socket for the butt of the rod.

251-pound tuna, and Mr. W. C. Boschen of New York in 1913 took a 335-pound swordfish (*Xiphias*), which is now the record fish of the Tuna Club and the world's record.

The reel used in this sport is large, generally an Edwin Vom Hofe make, and holds six hundred feet. Economy in tackle consists in buying the very best, and while a good outfit can be had for less money, the angler had better pay thirty or forty or more dollars for his reel, fifteen or twenty for the rod, and three or four for the line, as it will be put to the extreme test. The latest reels are as finely made as a watch and have abundant combinations—brakes, etc. The line for tuna or black sea bass should have a fine piano-wire leader eight or ten feet long, with several swivels, and the line for six or eight feet should be doubled. The hook is a No. 10 O'Shaughnessy, though if live bait is used it is smaller. If a flying fish or skipjack, it should be larger.

The rods are beautifully made, of split bamboo or noibwood, ironwood, greenheart, or hickory; have agate guides and just the right resiliency. The reel is set above the grip or between the butt and the left-hand grip, and should be on the upper side of the rod. The reel should always be *lashed* onto the rod, and the line should be run out and wet before fishing, as the friction will set a dry line afire, and line and hopes will go up in smoke. Sometimes a lead sinker is used to get the line down if the fish are low, as the salmon generally are at Monterey. The butt of such a rod is twenty-four inches long, with a tip seven feet long. On the silver tip of the butt fits a rubber pad, something like the rubber tips on a chair or crutch, but they come flat. In playing a large fish the angler should have a leather belt with a butt cap and use this as a fulcrum. All launches are rigged with a leather cap, fastened to the seat between the angler's knees. Nearly all the very large fish are caught from the seat fulcrum or base.

In this sea angling the tackle has a relation to the boat and is the result of evolution, the survival of the most desirable. The result is a perfect boat and perfect tackle, having in view absolute fair play and all the advantage on the side of the game.

The Santa Catalina boat is a launch eighteen or twenty feet long and wide of beam, built for safety, not for speed. An eight- or ten-horse power gasoline engine is placed amidships, and the wheel is on the right rail on the inside, so that the boatman, who is also the gaffer, can sit with his right hand on the wheel, his left on the bar of the engine. The anglers must sit side by side, facing the stern and in it; one fishes to the right, the other to the left, and when either has a strike the boatman stops the engine and the other angler reels in if it is desirable to give his friend the field. Then with the butt of his rod in the socket attached to the chair between his knees, the angler is in a position to play the largest game.

This is the so-called tuna tackle. Then comes what is popularly known as "9-9." The line is a number nine. The term "9" means that the line has nine threads or strands. Each strand having a breaking strength of two pounds; the entire line having a breaking strength of eighteen pounds. The rod must not weigh over nine ounces, nor can it be less than six feet in length. It is made of split bamboo, noibwood, greenheart, and various woods. A Shaver split bamboo "9-9" can be had for $20. It has agate guides and German silver mountings, and with it the angler can land a very large fish—up to one hundred pounds. Edwin Vom Hofe builds a "9-9" rod of noibwood which costs from $10 to $14. Any reel can be used, but usually a smaller one is employed that will hold 300 or 400 feet of No. 9 line.

Another grade of tackle in use by the Tuna Club in its tournaments, and invented by T. McD. Potter, a retired capitalist of Los Angeles, is known as "3-6." Here the rod weighs six ounces. The rod cannot be less than six feet; the line has 6 strands, and a breaking strength of twelve pounds, which explains the name "three-six"; viz., 6 feet, 6 strands, and 6 ounces. With this extraordinary rod, like a trout rod cut off, I saw Dr. Gifford Pinchot play a giant yellowtail five hours; and fishes up to sixty pounds, and doubtless over, are taken with it, the idea of the club being to prevent the slaughter of game fish; as it is impossible to land a fish on this tackle within fifteen minutes or half an hour, the result is most satisfactory.

The Tuna Club has a "sled" and a "kite"* which are employed with the tuna tackle. The former is to keep the bait away from the boat in trolling, while the kite makes the bait imitate the leap of the living flying fish when that lure is used. Tunas and swordfishes are often taken in this manner when they will not

* See pages 143 and 146

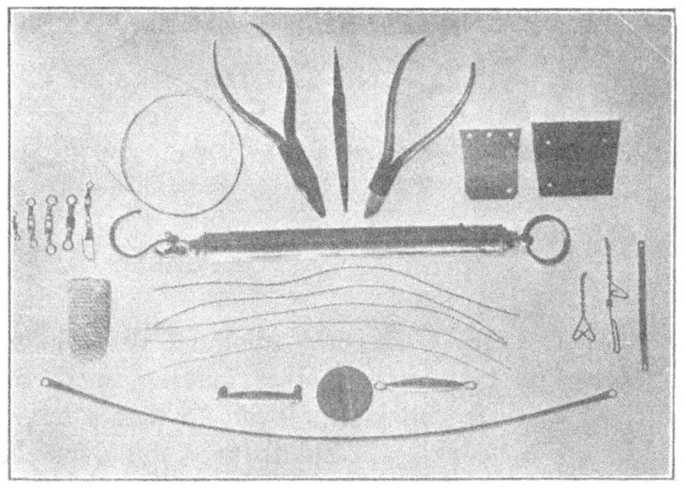

Equipment for the angling box

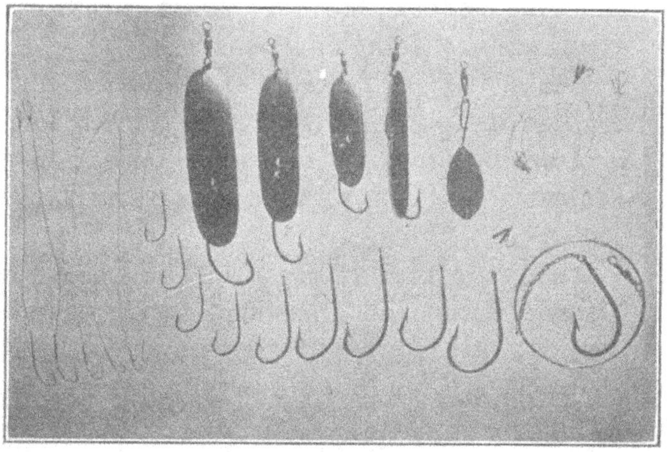

Hooks and spoons used in sea fishing

touch anything else. This tackle is now used at Aransas Pass in the Gulf of Mexico, where nearly all the tarpon are taken on the "9-9" tackle of the Tuna Club. As it is based on sportsmanship and humanitarian ideas, it is gradually spreading over the country where sea angling holds.

Surf casting, whether on the California or New Jersey coast, requires different methods, and a stiffer rod is employed so that a heavy bait can be cast a long distance out over the waves. The casting tackle on the Jersey coast for striped bass or channel bass is a stiff 16 ounce or over rod; the line a No. 24 or No. 30, according to the angler's taste.

The surf fish or roncador tackle on the sandy beaches of California, where the game is small or from one to three or four pounds, is a 9-ounce rod and No. 21 thread line or a No. 9 line.

Along the Florida coast and at Long Key Fishing Camp the all-around tackle used is tarpon tackle, so near the sixteen-ounce tackle of the Tuna Club that a description is unnecessary.

There are three general methods of angling deserving attention.

First.—Trolling, when the bait, generally a

fish or a bone jig or a spoon, is hauled or trolled after the boat from fifty to one hundred and fifty feet astern. If it is necessary to go fast, as for kingfish about Nassau, then a good pipe or wing sinker is needed to keep the bait down below the surface; but if the fish does not require speed to delude him, as in swordfish angling, a light one is used.

Second.—Still fishing. This in California is when the angler sights a school of fish—yellowtail or mackerel—and keeps them about the boat by (chumming) tossing over broken-up fish. Here the angler reels in his line and casts, long or short, as the case may be, with or without a sinker. This is one of the most fascinating methods in California, as the water is perfectly smooth and one can pick out the fish he wants.

Third.—Beach casting. Here the angler wades out into the surf with high boots or stands on the sands and casts. The rolling surf lends additional fascinaton to this method, which I have tried for the big Florida barracuda, channel bass, etc.

There is another method employed by thousands—that of wharf fishing, and Southern California has scores of angling piers along her coast, of no use for commerce, but patronized by anglers every day in the year. They use a long bamboo pole, with a stout line and many hooks, adapted to the height above the water. If a large fish is hooked the angler lowers down a grapnel and endeavors to hook the fish up, or gaff it. If it is too large to lift, it is led ashore and landed on the beach in the surf.

CHAPTER III

THE NEW ENGLAND GROUNDS

GROUP I

THE SWORDFISH
(*Xiphias*)

IT remained for the Tuna Club to put the swordfish of two species on the angling map as a game fish. The first *Tetrapturus* was taken with rod and reel by Mr. Llewellyn in 1896, and the first *Xiphias* by Mr. W. C. Boschen, a New York member, in 1913. The latter fish weighed 355 pounds and was one of three hooked by Mr. Boschen at Santa Catalina.

The *Xiphias,* like the tuna, is really a world-wide roamer, but is not common, and I think it varies according to season. The two localities where its catch can be depended upon, as a business, are south-eastern Massachusetts, around Block Island, and in the Mediterranean Sea, both, in all probability, spawning and feeding grounds for the fish.

Within the past ten years a number of specimens of *Xiphias* have been taken in nets or harpooned in southern California waters, and in 1913 the first one was taken with rod and reel. *Xiphias* is larger, heavier, and more bulky than *Tetrapturus*. It has a longer and wider sword and is more vicious. It attains a large size, running up to fourteen or fifteen feet, and a weight of one thousand pounds. Off the Massachusetts coast there is a fleet of schooners which follow it and bring scores into the market at Boston, where they command a good price as a market fish. They are all taken with a harpoon or lily-iron. The schooners sail about, keeping a man in the foretop, who, on seeing a fish lying on the surface with dorsal out of water, sings out, and the man at the helm runs for it. There is a "rest" or nest on the end of the jibboom, and here the harpooner stands and hurls or "jabs" his lily-iron as the jibboom moves over the fish. This swordfish is ugly and vicious, and many accidents have occurred, the fish sending its sword through the heaviest planks, smashing dories.

Up to date none of these fishes have been taken with a line in the Atlantic, but Dr. Gifford Pinchot hooked and played one four hours in 1912, when it broke the steel wire leader. This swordfish preys upon mackerel, dashing into a school, cutting the fishes down with its sword, then picking up the silvery pieces.

To try this game, either ship as a passenger on board one of the swordfish fishermen from Boston or go to Block Island or Santa Catalina and charter a cruising launch. When the fish is hooked get into a dory and play it to a finish, the launch following in case of accident.

Off Palm Beach and at Long Key Camp, Florida, there is an attractive little swordfish running up to 150 or so pounds. It rejoices in the title *Histiophorus,* and has an enormous dorsal fin, like a sail. This is a more or less common catch with tarpon tackle—a sixteen-ounce rod and a twenty-one or twenty-four line; but it can be, and should be, taken on "9-9." This fish is beautifully colored and leaps in joy in the blue waters of the Gulf Stream. There are one or two other swordfishes about Florida, where I have taken them with grains, but they are not common enough to mention.

The big *Xiphias* has left a long trail of devastation in its wake, of wrecked ships and boats. The most interesting was the case of the sloop "Red Hot." This vessel belonged to the U. S. Fish Commission; she was started upon a voyage of investigation, the *Xiphias* being one of the objectives, as at that time nothing was known of its young. The sword-fish tribe must have resented this. In any event, before she got well started, a big fellow rammed the "Red Hot," and, according to report, sent her to the bottom.

For some reason the Atlantic tuna and the Atlantic swordfish attain a larger size than in California waters. The Florida sharks are of two or three times greater bulk than the sharks of California. Perhaps it is the heat. The waters of Florida are very warm, while those of California are cool.

This difference in bulk has made this angling possible in California. The tunas here average about one hundred and fifty pounds, and six and eight hundred pounders are very rare. So with the *Xiphias*. The average in the Atlantic is a six- or eight-hundred-pound fish, almost impossible to the angler with rod and reel, while the same fish in the Santa Catalina channel averages two hundred and fifty pounds, the rod record, by Mr. Boschen, being 355 pounds.

In angling for *Xiphias*, as it is out at sea,

the fish should be hunted up, the tall dorsal fin being the beacon which it exposes when lying on the surface. Once found, the bait, a fresh mackerel, should be trolled across its path; the launch may go ahead and gradually slow down until the lure is just ahead. The line should have a ten-foot wire leader jointed with swivels at intervals. The hook should be generous—No. 10-12—and when the strike comes, the swordfish should be given time, as he has a hard, bony, toothless jaw, difficult to hook. When playing the fish from the dory it is well for the oarsman to be an observing person, as some years ago, off Long Island, a man was sitting in his dory when up through the bottom came four feet of a swordfish rapier, nearly spitting him. This, of course, will but add to the zest of the chase in the eyes of the sea angler. This fish is taken at Santa Catalina by using the kite invented by Captain George Farnsworth. By using this, the flying fish bait is made to leap—a proceeding which excites the big swordfish.

With the catching of this fish at Santa Catalina a new and exciting and risky sport has been discovered. The 355-pounder taken by Mr. Boschen repeatedly tried to ram the boat.

Group 2

THE POLLOCK AND ITS FRIENDS

IF I am not greatly mistaken, the finest of the inshore game fishes north of Cape Cod, the pollock, is neglected and not well known. We begin to hear of it north of Portsmouth, and at the entrance of some of the rivers knowing ones angle for it. I do not know very much about the fish, just enough to commend it to the light-tackle angler as a fine, sturdy game fish. I knew it best at Ogunquit, on the southeastern coast of Maine, where I fished for it from the rocks with my eight-ounce split bamboo trout or bass rod, using crab, lobster, shell, or fish bait. At the entrance of the little harbor, off the rocks, was the best ground, and here I made the discovery (to myself) that the pollock will take a fly. Doubtless someone else had made this wonderful discovery before, but it had not reached me, and one day, when I could find no crabs in the crevices, or was not active enough to catch them, I bethought me of a fly in my hatband, a relic of an angling trip to Blue Mountain Lake, in the Adirondacks, a few weeks previous.

It was a dilapidated Royal Coachman, but as I cast and it sank a foot, up rose a splendid five- or six-pound pollock and seized it. I was so surprised that I broke my tip on him, and confess that I broke two more tips on these Ogunquit pollocks before I learned that they were too big and heavy, too hard fighters, for my trout rod.

They made fine runs out to sea, nearly exhausting my reel; then would come in, like arrows from a bow, until they almost touched the rocks, to turn and dash away again, to the music of the reel, coming to the gaff or net only after a hard and splendid fight.

Use an eight-ounce trout or black bass rod, E line *not enameled* (raw silk); a small hook, No. 6 O'Shaughnessy; a triple-gut leader, and crab bait, if you must, but a fly if you are a sportsman.

So much for pollock, or coalfish, as the British Sea anglers call him. I know of fifty-four other names that he goes by, ranging from saithe to rock-salmon. All royalty are addicted to this multiplicity of names, and since the pollock, as we know him in America, is a royal fellow, he should be allowed a hundred names if he can get them. The fish has a wide range in Northern Europe, up as far as Spitzbergen, and has been taken in the Baltic. Its American range may be said to be from the mouth of the St. Lawrence to Nantucket. It is found in schools, generally on the surface, and in a general way has the habit of the bluefish, and its vigor. As a devourer of little fishes it is pre-eminent.

The pollock ranges up to ten pounds, and six pounds is a good average, explaining its strength on a trout rod. "Down East," or along the Maine coast and the Bay of Fundy, the fishermen call it the "quoddy salmon," and it affords fine sport from the rocks. In England the members of the British Sea Anglers' Society prize it highly as the coalfish, and there is an Alaskan species also called the coalfish by the Canadians. It comes south, and I have seen several specimens in the tanks of the Avalon, Santa Catalina, Aquarium. But it is rare and a straggler in these latter waters.

In my experience the pollock deteriorates very rapidly when taken from the water, and if it is not salted it should be eaten as soon as possible. I commend it as a fine fly-taking game fish.

When angling for pollocks you will take gurnards and sculpins, often ignorantly thrown away; but they are among the delicacies of the sea. The cod, hake, haddock, and halibut are taken in the deeper fields of the pollock, and a variety of small fry; also silver hake or whiting, the turbot, and the ling. The California hake is a good fish, taken by anglers in Monterey Bay when angling for salmon.

Porgy

Striped Bass

Bluefish

CHAPTER IV

NEW YORK AND NEW JERSEY GROUNDS

GROUP 3

THE STRIPED BASS AND ITS FRIENDS

ONE of the most successful instances of transplanting a fish is seen in the striped bass. The U. S. Fish Commission brought some striped bass to the Pacific coast some twenty years ago and placed them in the mouth of the Sacramento. They increased so rapidly that the fish is now one of the choice market fishes of California, a splendid addition to sport. Wanderers have reached Santa Catalina Island and Alamitos Bay, Los Angeles County, five hundred miles to the south.

The striped bass is one of the most beautiful of all fishes, pure silver with longitudinal stripes. In general appearance it is sturdy, the ideal game fish, attaining a length of five feet and a weight, under the most favorable conditions, of one hundred pounds.

"The stately Bass, old Neptune's fleeting Post
That tides it out and in from sea to coast."

This bass unquestionably has decreased in numbers during the past century on the Atlantic coast, as formerly it was a common fish near the St. Lawrence and particularly off New Bedford. The striped bass clubs that were formerly maintained on the southeast New England coast have in many instances been given up. The striped bass has practically disappeared or is much smaller. If the New Englander would find his old game, I would suggest the Asbury Park Fishing Club, as here, on the Jersey coast, the striped bass is still found in all its former splendor, and is taken by casting from the beach and wading out into the surf. In New England the bass anglers had iron docks built out from the rocks over the breaking sea and played their game from the stand, the gaffer standing on the rocks below. The rod used was a twelve-ounce split bamboo or some good wood, heavy and stiff for casting the lure—that *bonne bouche,* the tail of a lobster (when lobsters were five cents apiece and menhaden was the "chum"). I have seen forty-pound striped bass taken through the ice at Fishkill, Hudson River, in February, which suggests the dual nature of the striped bass—living in the ocean in summer, going up the rivers in winter, and living about their mouths at all times. In a word, they do not migrate or go south or off shore at the approach of winter, but remain in one general location all the time. They are more or less gregarious in their food, lobster, clam, and crab ranking first; but I have taken them with menhaden and fish bait, and while crustaceans are the game of their choice, they will chase small fishes, as minnows, squid and shrimp, into the breakers. The striped bass spawns in May and June, often in rivers, but doubtless also at sea. The record rod fish, so far as known, is one taken at Cuttyhunk, weighing 104 pounds. A 112-pounder, nearly six feet in length, was taken at Orlean, Mass., with a harpoon.

The striped bass is the embodiment of power and strength, and when played, as at Cuttyhunk, from a pier chair, with the butt of the rod in a belt, with waves breaking all about, the sport is of a stimulating, exciting character. Pasque and Cuttyhunk of the Elizabeth Islands, between Buzzard's Bay and Martha's Vineyard, were formerly fine localities. The members of the Asbury Park Fishing Club still find this fish in fair quantities and have famous sport along the coast wading out and casting, taking the game amid surroundings calculated to arouse a fine sporting spirit.

In San Francisco the striped bass is the game fish of the region. It has increased so that it is found all over the great bay and up in the flats, where it is taken trolling and still fishing. Specimens of eighteen or twenty pounds are not uncommon.

On the Atlantic coast is found the sea bass, "Another gentleman among his finny comrades," according to Frank Forester. This bass is a dark, leaden-hued fellow, with a light dorsal fin and a filament extending out from the upper tip of its tail. Like many fishes, it has many names, but where I have known it best—Fisher's Island and vicinity—it was the sea bass. Rock bass, blackwill, hannahell, blue-fish are other names, but sea bass suits it best. I frequented the dulcet waters near the entrance to the Sound for the bluefish, and we took our bass with black bass tackle, an eight-ounce split bamboo, and lobster or crab for bait.

A large sea bass is a very powerful fish, affording the angler sport, exercise, and entertainment of a varied character. This fish has a wide range. I have taken it in Massachusetts, Virginia—at Old Point Comfort, in Florida, and I am told that it has been caught at Aransas Pass, Texas. I have also seen it it off Madison, Conn., and it has a habit of hovering about certain points or ledges. It is not a large or startling fish, but a good fighter. A pound or two is the average, and five or six pounds is a good fish. If I am not mistaken, I have seen ten-pounders brought into Madison. But I was not the angler, and I was "guessing."

The sea bass is the fish of the people of New York, and steamers go out to the bass banks with crowds, lined up and down the rail, to angle for them. Many anglers pursue the sport, and no other, and have been at it half a century. These anglers use a short, thickset club rod, made for the purpose, and a big reel, often an English "wood winch," as the bass are taken in deep water. When the steamer finds the place off Long Branch she stops; the sea bass soon begin to come in and are hoisted out of the deeps.

The fishing ground is Cholera Banks, about twenty miles from Sandy Hook. Another favorite ground extends from off Navesink down the coast as far as Squam. This is fishing, in contradistinction to angling. The water is fifty, sixty or more feet deep, so a heavy sinker is essential, taking the lure down quickly to the region of sea bass, blackfish, fluke, rock cod, porgy, weakfish, and many more, by whom a hard clam or menhaden bait is not to be despised. At Charleston, South Carolina, there is a smaller species of sea bass, and here the angler may take the beautiful squirrel-fish, also of the sea bass tribe. The tautog or blackfish is often confused with the sea bass, as both are called blackfish in certain parts of Long Island Sound. One, the tautog or chogset, is a very different fish and a kinsman of the beautiful parrot-fishes of the South. Certain species were greatly esteemed by the ancient Greeks and Romans. "Brains of Jove," Numa called the scarus. In a general way the fish ranges in shallow water from New Brunswick to South Carolina, being the fish of the people in New England, where it is known as the tautog, a Narragansett word, but in New York it is the blackfish, in Virginia the chub, in the Carolinas the oyster-fish.

When I was a boy this fish was taken in great numbers from the Red and Nahant rocks with long bamboo poles. The small fishes were called "nippers," a term which should apply to the real nippers; and nipper parties, in which ladies and whole families took part, near "Tudors," were the vogue. A long slender bamboo rod to reach out over the water, a light line, small hook, and almost any bait will lure this fish, which makes a vigorous fight when given fair play with light tackle. It is a game little fish from half a pound up to two or three, occasionally more, and one of the best edible fishes of New England.

"When chestnut leaves are as big as thumbnails,
Then bite blackfish without fail;
But when chestnut leaves are as large as a span,
Then catch blackfish if you can."

In other words, the tautog is a summer fish, but does not go far from its haunts in winter.

The chogset, cunner or bergall, is a summer fish, and under the title of nipper is taken from the Nahant, Lynn, and Cape Ann rocks, as in the case of the sea bass. Back in the seventies I spent the summer on the Maine coast, near Mouse Island. As only one fish was to be had from the rocks, we organized the Nipper or Cunner Club, and Dan Beard and I fought piscatorial battles for the presidency.

The nipper (*Ctenolabrus*) is a long, slender, light-green little fish, with a long sea bass-like dorsal. It swims by its pectoral fins, like the parrot-fishes, and has an inordinate passion for soft clams; hence anyone can take it on light tackle, and it is a very delicious little fish.

My first angling was had on Red Rock, Lynn, standing among the flying spume, when the sea was on, fishing for nippers, gradually retreating, as the tide rose, before the great waves which, at the flood, often drove us to the land. Fried cunners cooked in the old Nahant fashion ought to go down the ages with white bait, Santa Catalina sand-dabs, and the murries of Cæsar.

Group 4

THE CHANNEL BASS, PORGY, ETC.

ONE of the finest game fishes in American waters is the channel bass, or red drum; just as game by any other name, and he has one for every State from New York to Texas, and some to spare. I have angled for him off Asbury Park, N. J., at Old Point Comfort, in the entrance to the St. Mary's, in Georgia with fiddler-crab bait, at the mouth of the St. John's, at Mayport, where the ebb tide is so violent that my heavy sinker floated, and again in shallow pools inside Aransas Pass, Texas, and everywhere the fish is game, good, and wholly acceptable if not murdered on heavy tackle.

The channel bass may be known at once by the spot on his tail like a big period. Randolph describes him in verse as

> "Long as a salmon, if not so stout,
> And springy and swift as a mountain trout."

The fish has a superficial resemblance to the salmon, and has a very wide range in many waters. He is a bottom-loving fish; hence is found in the surf along sandy beaches, and is one of the great game fishes of the famous Asbury Park Club. In Florida I found good fishing in the St. John's River, at the mouth, using fiddler-crabs for bait, a nine-ounce split bamboo rod, a No. 9 line, and triple-gut leader. I had the promise of a fifty-pounder and caught one of twenty or thirty pounds, and a harder fighting fish it would be difficult to find. The moment I had a strike, out into the stream would go the fish, plunging down and up, in and out, in a series of gyrations which, when taken in conjunction with the tide, made hard work.

The best fishing for this game creature is on the Jersey coast, in the surf, where the anglers wade in and with stiff rods cast far out into the boiling water. A No. 21 or a No. 24 linen line is the thing for this work, a good multiplying reel, a 10/0 hook, and fairly heavy sinker. Clam or crab bait is commended by experts. At Old Point Comfort I used soft shell crabs, " shedders," which old Sandy used to peddle around at two-bits a dozen, yelling at his mule, " W'at I feed yo' fo'? "

Surf fishing on the Jersey Coast

The Jersey anglers speak of the fish as the channel bass, but in Texas he is the drum. The term drum comes from the sound the fish makes, due to its curious air-bladder. In Texas I found the fish in holes in shallow water, often among the reeds or tulles, and here shrimp was the bait, or young mullet.

There is a certain amount of expectancy in this sport, as one always hopes to hook the one-hundred-pounder that is said to have been seen, but fifty pounds is large for the fish and the average is under twenty pounds. In appearance the channel bass is very attractive, as its upper scales are bronzed and often of a deep-red hue. Some fishes have two spots instead of one. In the same general localities the angler will find the black drum fish, which attains a weight of eighty or more pounds. The banded drum fish is the young of this species.

The sheepshead is an interesting fish that wanders up to twenty or more pounds in old specimens, and with its twelve or thirteen black and white vertical stripes is very attractive, while its high-domed shape makes it a hard fighter. It has a very wide range from Block Island to the Rio Grande. I believe I have taken it in every State alongshore; but, as I recall it, Florida holds the palm for numbers. I have had my best sport with this fish with an eight-ounce rod, eight or more feet in length.

In angling for these fishes the true game qualities are lost by the use of heavy and really unreasonable tackle or hand lines. A five-pound fish has no chance on a sixteen-ounce rod, any more than a one-pound trout on a nine-ounce rod.

Group 5

THE WEAKFISH AND OTHERS

ON the New England coast most of the well-known fishes were given Indian names. One, the squeteague, is one of the most appreciated fishes in the country, as its family or allies include some of the really great game fishes of the world, from the weakfish of New York and the great white sea bass of California to the Kabeljou of Cape Colony. All and many more belong to the clan *Cynoscion.*

The majority of anglers who go down New York bay a-fishing, are weakfish anglers. You may find the species *nobile* from New York to the Gulf of Mexico, and everywhere it is a fine fish appealing alike to the angler and the epicure. It is called " sea-trout," as it looks very much like a lusty steelhead trout, with its silvery sides and fine spots; and in its best condition the fish is not far behind this great game fish of the sea and river.

Each state on the Atlantic seaboard glories in the possession of this fish, and each has a different name for it. Around Nantucket it is the drummer. President Cleveland and Joe Jefferson fished for "yellow-fin" in Buzzard's Bay. At Old Point, Virginia, my boatman took me out after bluefish. In Georgia my man gave me sea-trout; on the St. Mary's "spot." But it was all the same fish, the squeteague or weakfish. When the bluefish season is a great success the weakfish are not out in force, or *vice versa.* I have often been told this, and it may be that it is not so; but the two fishes have very much the same habit though the bluefish is the hardest fighter.

Professor Baird wrote of the weakfish as follows: "The sport of catching the Squeteague is very great, and is highly enjoyed by many fishermen, on account of the great number that can be taken in a very short time. They swim near the surface and require a line but little leaded. They take almost any kind of bait, especially clams, soft crabs or pieces of fish. They take the hook with a snap, rarely condescending to nibble, and constant vigilance is necessary, as well as extreme care in hauling them out of the water, on account of the extreme tenderness of the mouth. During the flood tide they keep in the channel-ways of the bays, and at the ebb they generally settle in some deep hole, where they remain until the flood entices them out again. In the night they are much in the habit of running up the creeks in the salt meadows, where they are sometimes taken in great numbers by interposing between them and the sea, just before the period of high water. This experiment is not very satisfactory on the coast of New Jersey, in consequence of the abundance of crabs. The smaller fish become gilled in the net-meshes, thus inviting the attacks of the crabs, which cut the nets to pieces, often ruining them in a single night."

I have had ideal sport at the old fort at the entrance of the St. Mary's River. Between the town and the fort is a fiddler-crab town, and not far away sea-trout are found, affording splendid sport. I have also taken them in the St. John's at Mayport and Pilottown. I well remember the porgies, fine sea-trout, the big channel bass, and the enormous sharks I hooked from the beach, with the Minorcans, near Pilottown, and one day a huge sunfish sailed into the river and ran aground on the bar where we wrecked it, after the fashion of the country. (1876).

The bluefish is occasionally found with the squeteague, sometimes as a boon companion, and again as a pursuer and false friend. It can truly be said that the bluefish is the finest game fish of the sea in New England waters, and that it is thoroughly game, and a hard and fierce contestant. Its entire appearance indicates the game fish, strength, agility and quickness, and when we add to these qualifications ferocity we have the bluefish, one of the hardest fighters in the Seven Seas.

The bluefish is blue above and silver below. His eye is big, lustrous and beautiful. When he sweeps in out of the unknown, an invading, exterminating army, the whole country knows it, as aside from being a game fish *par excellence,* it is a dish from the gods when broiled just out of the water. Years ago when I went to Fisher's Island to try the bluefish with rod and reel I lived at a little inn near the landing, where the attraction was the negro cook who specialized on bluefish. The fish were caught hardly six hundred feet distant, rushed in, and I was awakened by hearing them flopping about in the wheelbarrow as my man wheeled them up.

This was the signal to rise, and half an hour later to the dot came, "Bluefish am served, sah!" I was there, and if the envious shade of Lucullus was not hovering about I am greatly mistaken. My Yankee taste may be perverted, but bluefish, fresh mackerel, shad shad roe, and Atlantic salmon, are in a class by themselves, and if the angling reader does not know them fresh, as above, he has never eaten them at their best.

The bluefish is found well distributed over the globe, a wanderer in many seas, but it arrives in New England in May or June and remains until October; its movements, to some extent, depending upon those of the menhaden, its natural prey. The bluefish apparently does not like water colder than 40°, nor is it at home in the Tropics. In the cold months it probably goes to some offshore deep-water-ground as it slopes into the deep Atlantic. The fishes are subject to singular migrations and appear in a certain place one year and do not visit the locality again for ten years. Off Block Island, the entrance to Long Island Sound, around Nantucket, is a summer home of the fish, and here hundreds of fishermen enjoy the sport of trolling for bluefish in catboats, with a handline and jig. The fresh breeze, the blue water, the pure air, the overpowering strength of the fish makes the sport exciting and in a class by itself.

The bluefish is one of the finest rod catches

known. It ranks with the California yellowtail. The Santa Catalina Island launches should be introduced in the East as they are seaworthy and made to meet the exact requirements of the bluefish, which has many of the habits of the yellowtail. Usually the boat is anchored, and menhaden (chum) chopped fine are thrown over to attract them. The angler may use his taste regarding rods, but a nine-ounce rod eight feet long, with a 9 line and No. 10/0 hook, with piano-wire leader is sufficient as the fish does not run over fifteen pounds and the average fish weighs about seven or eight. A strip of menhaden, a bone jig, a pearl jig, or any small fish is used.

Around New York the young bluefish are favorites among anglers, who call them snappers and take them with a trout rod, No. 6 linen line, click reel, No. 4 hook. The little fishes make a remarkable fight.

CHAPTER V

THE FLORIDA GROUNDS

GROUP 6

THE BIG BARRACUDA

WHEN the angler arrives in Florida, as he now can with the ease and comfort of well-equipped Pullman cars, he finds among the marine game fishes a long slender fish that calls to mind the muscallunge. It is the big barracuda, the muscallunge of the sea, a totally different fish, but just as game, a fierce, and hard fighter. Barracudas can be found all over the world, but this species, (*Sphyraena barracuda*) is a giant running up to sixty or seventy pounds, more or less, and from four to six feet in length; in his prime condition calculated to give the angler a splendid contest. In appearance he looks the piratical part he plays on the Florida reef. He is a wrecker, a cannibal. He is greenish above, silvery below, with big black eyes, a long rakish jaw filled with sharp fang-like teeth. He might be a shark, and, according to Jordan, is in some waters, a menace to bathers.

If the angler goes down to the sea with a rope or a club rod for this fish he may be disappointed; also the fish will not shine as a fighter if taken on a big cod-line on a bone jig, though if he is big enough and the launch is going too fast he will almost pull a man out of a boat. But if one goes out with a nine-ounce seven-foot rod, with just the right sort of resiliency to give the fish fair play, yet lift him; if a No. 9 line and a No. 10 hook, with mullet bait or some shiny fish is used and the game is played from a dinghy or small boat, the angler will have the time of his life with the big barracuda.

I am told that great numbers are taken at Long Key Camp and all along the upper Florida coast, but my home was at Garden Key, Tortugas, sixty miles beyond Key West, where the big fish lived in the deep blue channels and the smaller ones on the shallow reef. Here I waded for them with my light tackle and enjoyed the true delights of barracuda angling, though I am not throwing cold water on the big fish which I took in the channels trolling. The argument I make is, that more sport

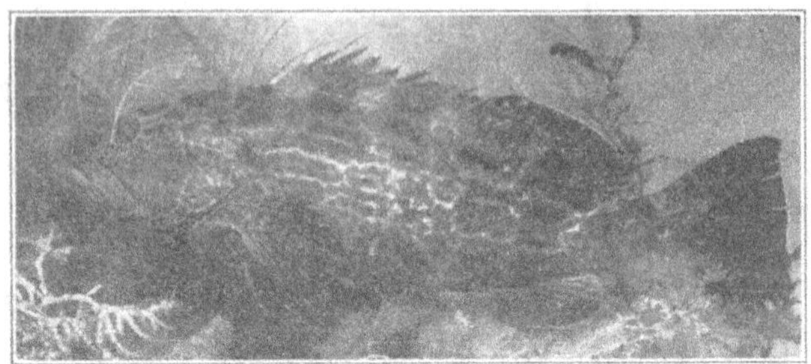

Black Grouper

Hogfish

Great Barracuda

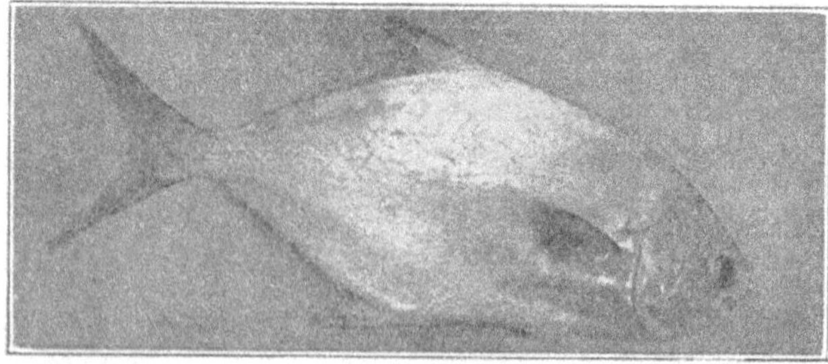

Pompano

is had from a dinghy or small boat, where the fish has a chance to pull his enemy overboard and reduce his pride.

Nearly all fishes will sound when hooked in deep water, and the angler must pump them up, whether it be tuna, black sea bass or bluefish. But on a shallow reef, where the water was not over ten feet deep and mostly four feet, I played the ten and twenty-pound barracudas and found them the finest of fighters. Five and six-pounders are often found in the shallows, and I commend for them an eight-ounce trout rod with live bait.

This Florida fish, (and he ranges all over the Gulf region) in a general way, is a solitary; that is, he is not found in a school, and to see and watch him, as I have many times, sneak up on a school of mullet is worth while. He stalks them as a tiger does its prey, and plays with the victim as a cat will a mouse. I have seen a young barracuda catch a sardine by the tail and hold it ten minutes without moving, apparently to enjoy its struggles.

The California barracuda, *S. argentea,* is caught in great numbers in the Santa Catalina channel, in schools. It comes in from the outer sea in April or May in vast schools; in a sense, breaks up, and is found with yellowtail, and is caught in the same manner—with a nine-ounce rod, number nine line though the 3-6 tackle, previously referred to, is the best. I have taken these fish at twelve or fifteen pounds and had what might be termed sport; but on heavier tackle the fish soon gives up and displays an amiable desire to come aboard. It is only fair, however, to this barracuda, to say that he is nearly always taken when angling for larger game and considered a nuisance. If the angler is using very light tackle he will find the fish better than nothing, and as an edible fish he ranks with the first fish families of California.

Another small species of barracuda *Sphyraena borealis* is found along the South Atlantic coast, but rarely caught or seen by the average angler. The British sea anglers off Cape Town include among their game fishes a small barracuda, and off Portugal one hears of Aflalo catching the " bicuda," probably a cousin of our grim, ugly fellow of the Florida and Bahama reefs.

Group 7

SAILFISH AND AMBER-JACK

WE read of the Paradise of the angler, and the writer, who really loves fishing, falls into the habit of calling every place where he has had good luck a paradise. Along comes a victim, lured by the description and has the antipodes of this luck and does not see where the description fits. But Florida, and the Santa Catalina channel, including San Clemente, California, may truthfully be given this term, due to the great variety of fishes and the splendid sport to be had.

The Tuna Club, as stated in a previous chapter, now counts the swordfish in the class with the tuna and admits anglers who take a fish weighing 200 pounds with rod and reel to their active membership list. They have a swordfish insignia which the victorious angler can wear if he is so disposed, all of which suggests not vain display, but the respect with which the swordfish is held by these veterans of the rod and reel.

In Florida there are three distinct species

of swordfish,* one of which belongs to the Santa Catalina genus (*Tetrapturus imperator*). Another is known as the Cuban swordfish (*Tetrapturus amplus*), which I have taken with the grains after a hard fight; while the third (*Istiophorus nigricans*), is the common catch of the reef and of the anglers at Long Key Camp, upper Florida, and is a relative of the great sailfish of the Indian Ocean, which attains a length of twenty or thirty feet and has a dorsal fin that when erect resembles the sail of a boat painted after the Venetian fashion. These magnificent fish are harpooned by the natives of Madagascar and often wreck the boats and kill the men. An American consul saw one leap through the sail of a native proa—and described the flight to me.

The fish in Florida is called spearfish, sailfish, aguja voladora and by other names, but it is a swordfish, and like its African cousin, has a magnificently colored fin nearly as long as the fish and rising like a sail above it. Here the resemblance ceases as it rarely attains a weight of two hundred pounds, the average being one hundred, which makes it a good game fish for the rod and reel.

The fish appears to like the warm waters of

* Some are called sailfishes, others spearfishes, but all are really swordfishes in the use of their weapon.

the Gulf Stream as they sweep up the coast and are often found in schools. Down the reef (Tortugas) they are not so common, nor have I ever noticed them in very shallow water. The approved method is to anchor, as at Palm Beach, off the pier, and cast with live bait or troll from a launch. The tackle should be a 9-ounce, 6 or 8-foot rod, No. 9 line, or if desirable the typical old-fashioned tarpon tackle, a 16-ounce rod and No. 24 line; to use a larger line would be to take an unfair advantage of the game.

The fish is very active, a great jumper at all times, and when hooked makes a savage play about the boat, folding its big fin flat; but sometimes when hooked in deep water it erects this sail and to lift the fish against it is a most back-breaking operation. With a "9-9" tackle a one hundred-pound fish should be taken in less than thirty minutes. Every day in season these fishes are taken off Palm Beach and other localities, especially at Long Key Camp, in the center of a wonderful angling region.

Caught in the same waters and under similar conditions is the Florida yellowtail or amberjack. It is a typical Santa Catalina yellowtail, only heavier and deeper, this and other peculiarities making it a totally different species. The California fish is longer, more slender, more graceful and attractive, and known as *Seriola dorsalis* from its long dorsal fin. The Florida species is *Seriola lalandi.* It is one of the finest of all game fishes; fights to a finish; is not caught until it is in the boat, and is a master of strategy, finesse and bulldog strength. Fifty, sixty or eighty pounders are taken off the coast, and if the angler uses fair tackle he will have the time of his life. Specimens of this fish have been taken weighing nearly one hundred pounds. The largest specimens will be six feet in length, a ponderous game to handle on any tackle.

Ideal fishing for amber-fish is that from a drifting rowboat or a boat held by the oarsman and allowed to drift; but often, as at Palm Beach, the boat is anchored beyond the surf. If large fish are desired it is better to use a tarpon rod, sixteen ounces, and No. 21 line and No. 10 hook, with live mullet or some attractive fish. The amber-fish is also taken trolling. The angler should wear a leather socket belt, if a light rod is used, into which he can insert the butt of the rod, and stand and play the fish. If a heavy rod is employed he should have a socket screwed onto the seat; this is necessary in playing a large fish though of course the butt can be placed under the leg. A good contrivance when using the light rods, advocated in this book, is the flat rubber tip for the butt of the rod. In using this the angler can stand in the boat and press the rubber against the body and employ it as a fulcrum. In all these rods the reel is on the upper side and above the right hand grip, and has a left hand smaller grip of cork or cord above the reel.

If the weather permits, the angler who goes outside of Biscayne Bay should insist on a light boat being towed or carried, and when the amber-fish are found, at Fowey Rock Light or elsewhere, the angling should be done from the small boat, or the angler can sit in the small boat facing the stern, his boatman at the oars, ready. When the strike comes (assuming that they are trolling from a launch) the painter is cast off and the fish is played from the small boat.

The amber-fish has the habit of a number of large fishes, as the yellowtail, white sea bass and others. It will lie beneath a school of anchovies, sardines, or bluefish, and while it does not appear to molest them if the angler will drop his hook into the throng and can hook one of the small fry, it is almost certain that the amber-fish will take it. Few if any of the Florida fishes makes the splendid and vigorous play of this silver, green and yellow game.

GROUP 8

THE SMALL GAME FISHES OF FLORIDA

IN drifting over the Florida reef from Loggerhead to the St. John's the angler is always finding some new and interesting game, and a volume could be filled with descriptions of them. Two interesting fishes impress themselves on the memory. One is the lady fish, *Albula vulpes,* found also in California. This fish can be taken trolling or still fishing, and it requires very fine tackle though it attains a length of three feet and a weight of twelve pounds. It is a long slender, slippery, sardine-like fish, built something like a tarpon, with a powerful tail which enables it to take stupendous leaps often amazing the angler.

The other fish is the ten-pounder, *Elops saurus;* a silvery, long-headed fish which also attains a length of three feet or so and maximum and not unusual weight of ten pounds. To catch the fish it is well to hunt out some one who knows its particular haunts, as it is a weird creature, often found coming in onto shallow flats with the flood-tide, its big dorsals out of the water, yet so timid that the slightest noise will alarm it.

A good stiff eight-ounce split bamboo black-bass rod ten feet in length is the tackle, with a No. 6 line if you wish to give the game fair play. The hook should be a No. 3/0 or No. 4/0 with a long double or twisted gut leader. The bait of its liking is fiddlers, spirit crabs or even the red grapsus, or the soldier crab, and I have taken them with crayfish. They come in like mullet, in schools, but not stirring up the mud, and when hooked, they make a splendid, even remarkable play for so small a fish. Gregg gives Norris Cut, Bears Cut, Soldier Key and various passes as good localities on the east coast.

These two fishes will afford the angler no end of pleasure, as to take them requires skill and prescience of the angling variety, and they never will be taken unless the angler knows something about their habits. By this I mean that an angler could not learn to take a ten-pounder from a "correspondence school" or from a book. He must find out from some one who knows where they are found and then watch them.

There are scores of grunts in Florida waters, charming little fishes if taken with light tackle. Then come the snappers,—mangrove, gray, red and many more; beautiful fishes calling to mind the black bass, having all its game qualities and beauty. The red snapper I would not include as a game fish as it is taken only in deep water. The king of the snappers from the angling standpoint is the gray snapper, *Lutianus griseus,* to my mind one of the most attractive of all fishes and certainly the cleverest, and in my experience the most difficult to catch. I fished for it daily for several years, winter and summer, on the extreme outer Florida reef, hence this opinion is based on mature experience.

In weight the gray snapper runs up, though rarely, to twenty pounds; the average catch is from three to six pounds. A six-ounce split bamboo with a No. 6 line, small but stout hook, sardine or crayfish bait. I used a very fine copper leader three or four feet long that would settle in the sand, and often took them by manipulating the bait. When the gray snapper is hooked it makes an incomparable play, if one remembers that it must have light tackle.

With the snappers I would class the beautiful little yellowtail, *Ocyurus chrysurus,* a dainty little creature ranging up to three or four pounds. I always found it outside the breakers in groves of coral and gorgonias or sea fans. A five-ounce trout rod is fair for this fine little game fish that is known as the *rabirubia* at Key West and which is one of the delicious pan fishes of the region, a hard fighter and gallant game.

With the yellowtail comes the angel- and parrot-fishes, all brilliant and beautiful. Both must have a very small but very strong hook as the parrot-fish particularly will bite off the shank of the average hook. These wonderful fishes—the black angel, the green parrot—make a remarkable play and will repay the angler. If he is told they will not bite he must disregard it and use hooks advised, and discover two of the finest of the small game fishes of Florida.

There is another yellowtail caught here, *Bairdiella chrysura,* also the *Catalineta* or bandfish, and the sumptuous porgy (*Calamus*) of several kinds, and the little bream (*Lagodon*) are all game fishes if taken with light rods.

One of the most sturdy of all these fishes is the tripletail, *Lobotes,* which is taken up to ten or twelve pounds. No. 9 line, No. 4 hook, shrimp or crab bait. This fish has a wide range, and at times is common in the Chesapeake Bay where thirty pounders have been caught by anglers.

The common chub, *Kyphosus,* is no mean game. It has a very small mouth, which explains why so few are taken with rod and reel as grunt and snapper hooks are altogether too large for it and a very small No. 2 hook, but stout, should be used, and a small bait, the red meat of crayfish preferred. I have taken this fish up to eight pounds and include it, so far as my own experience goes, with the finest of the game fishes. It has no little individuality and swims with a vigorous and powerful movement of the tail.

One of the most interesting of the Florida fishes is the large mouth, brilliantly colored hogfish, *Lachnolaimus falcatus,* the courtier of the reef. It is a fine game fish when treated properly; that is, caught with light tackle, a six-ounce rod and a No. 6 line, a large hook No. 5, crayfish bait. It is also one of the fine table fishes of Florida. In appearance it is most striking; a brilliant red color, its three first dorsal spines very long, and all its fins long and exaggerated.

I have always found the fish in rather deep

water in coral patches on the sides of channels. A ten-pounder will be a revelation to the man with a rod, though the average fish is not over four pounds.

I can wish the angler with light tackle no better game than the pompano, which is found here in great numbers, and whether on the line or on the table, is a joy forever.

GROUP 9

THE TARPON

THE tarpon, owing to its high and lofty jumping habits, is one of the best known of the marine game fishes. It is a giant herring and looks the part. Its large scales, five inches across, its extraordinary mouth, its big eyes, near the top of the head, its mail of silver, are all features that add to its spectacular appearance.

The tarpon ranges up to four hunderd pounds and attains a length of seven feet or so. It is a migratory fish and in great bands moves up and down the Atlantic coast of North America from the northern coast of South America, British and Dutch Guiana to New York, its northern limit for numbers being the St. John's River. For many years the habits of the tarpon were unknown, but it is now known to winter in the Panuco River in the vicinity of Tampico, Mexico, and doubtless in many other streams. Here it is found in vast numbers and affords fine sport. In early spring

Tarpon

it begins to move north, arriving at Aransas Pass, Texas, in April or May, affording excellent sport at the Tarpon Club in the pass up to November when it goes south to winter.

The tarpon reaches Florida and the other Gulf localities about the same time and enters the rivers where it is supposed to spawn. As to this nothing is really known, but a few of the very young have been seen in rivers in Porto Rico. It is known that the adult tarpon will spend months in the summer in fresh water and in springs at the head of rivers (Florida).

At all times the tarpon readily takes fish bait, mullet or sardine, and as it is, as a rule, caught in shallow water it leaps and affords magnificent sport. It is taken by fishing on the bottom (still fishing) or by trolling (dragging the bait). The modern tackle, devised by the Tuna Club, and introduced at Aransas Pass by Mr. L. P. Streeter, is a nine-ounce, six- or seven-foot rod, a No. 9 line; the leader, of piano-wire with links of brass swivels, is fastened to a No. 10 hook. The bait is a half or whole mullet—the *bonne bouche* of the tarpon.

The first tarpon I hooked at Port Aransas, I had out not over twenty or thirty feet of line; yet the fish took it and when hooked went into the air higher than my head, so I was obliged to look up, and over my right shoulder to see this swinging dervish of a fish high in air.

How high a tarpon will leap I do not know, but ten or fifteen feet up and thirty horizontally would not be too much to accord it, and I have seen ten high successive leaps. All, or nearly all the photographs of tarpon seen are forced or the result of holding the fish on a short hand-line and photographing it from the same or another boat, and are more or less facsimiles of the legitimate leap when on the No. 9 line, and nine-ounce rod.

Tarpon fishing is found at Tampico in winter; Port Aransas in summer, Galveston and at many of the Gulf of Mexico or Florida resorts, as Boca Grande, Sarasola, Useppa Island, Long Key, St. Petersburg, Punta Rassa, Fort Meyers, and other places in Florida.

The tarpon is more dangerous than a shark, as should it land in a boat after a wild leap the wise angler would take to the water to escape the terrific blows of the silver-scaled tail, sufficient to break a man's back or leg. Methods differ in different localities and the angler will do well to secure the services of the best guide or boatman and take his advice entirely until he has mastered the art of curbing a 150-

pound "silver king" with a nine-ounce rod and a No. 9 line.

There are three angling clubs which make a speciality of tarpon: the Izaac Walton Club of Useppa Island, Florida, the St. Petersburg, Florida, Tarpon Club and the Tarpon Club of Port Aransas on the Texan coast. The latter club was founded by Mr. L. P. Streeter, secretary of the Tuna Club of Santa Catalina Island, who went to Texas to introduce the fair play light tackle of the Tuna Club. He demonstrated that heavy rods and lines are not necessary, and to-day the great game fish is taken with rods and lines described, and beautiful cups and trophies are offered for the winners in the various classes which are sport. When the first vessels are passing the Panama Canal an attempt will be made by California anglers to float a one hundred-foot car filled with tarpon from the Gulf of Mexico into the Pacific Ocean. It is estimated that tarpon would swim north as far as Santa Catalina Island and possibly the Bay of Monterey.

Group 10

THE JEWFISH AND BLACK GROUPER

ONE would hardly include the great Florida jewfish among the game fishes, yet it affords a certain amount of sport at times on the rod. It is an entirely different fish from the black sea bass of Santa Catalina, being a big ungainly grouper living on the bottom preferably in mud holes. The maximum weight is six or eight hundred pounds, and I have heard of goliaths that reached one thousand pounds. It is found all along the coast of the Mexican Gulf and in the Bahamas, and is known as Junefish, guasa, mero and by other names, and is the *Promicrops gansa* of science. The young are attractive fishes of a light olive-green tint fading into yellow, with darker crossbar, usually five in number. The adult is often very dark, or greenish black, and may be six or more feet in length; a colossus that requires shark tackle though a big fellow can be worn out with tuna tackle.

The small fishes, under twenty pounds, af-

Jewfish

ford fair sport with rod and reel. The tail of the jewfish is rounded outward; its mouth is enormous, the eyes near the upper part of the skull, the body big and clumsy. At Aransas Pass it is often fished for at night with rod and reel off the beach. The large jewfish is tough and impossible, only the young being of use for the camp or table.

The grouper family is a large and important one in Florida and is on the ragged edge of the aristocrats of the real game fishes; but there are a number of cousins of the groupers that are extremely attractive fishes. The common red grouper is a deep-water fish by taste, but is found on the edge of reefs and so often taken in upper Florida when trolling. Down the reef it is taken with hand-lines in water from thirty to sixty or more feet. It is a large lusty fish, ranging from ten to seventy pounds. The one that, in my estimation, and I have caught them all, is really a game fish, is the so-called black grouper (*Garrupa nigrita*), also called jewfish (*Mero de lo alto*) and by other names. It has a square tail, enormous head, high dorsals, large eye, and presents a more shipshape appearance than the jewfish. In a word, it looks like a hard fighting game fish, which it is. It is a chocolate-brown in color, adapting itself, more or less, to the reef (Key West portion), but well repays the angler. It lives in the clear water and has more the habit of the black sea bass which it resembles. A sixteen-ounce, six or seven-foot rod, No. 21 or No. 24 line, is sufficiently strong, and the bait may be fish or crayfish; if the latter, the whole tail, (shelled).

The Nassau grouper or hamlet, the red grouper, speckled hind, red hind, rock hind or spotted grouper, are all attractive fishes ranging the Florida region and the Bahamian banks many of them fine fishes when they can be taken with rod and reel.

CHAPTER VI

THE GULF GROUNDS

Group II

THE KINGFISH AND ITS ALLIES—SPANISH MACKEREL, ETC.

IN the Gulf of Mexico and the Straits of Florida a typical sea muscallunge is found in the kingfish; a long lithe giant, Spanish mackerel-like fish, one of the important food fishes of the South and affording the finest kind of sport when it can be taken with rod and reel.

Almost any time in approaching Key West the steamer will pass a fleet of boats fishing for kingfish. The fish, *Scomberomorus cavalla,* ranges from ten to one hundred pounds, and from fifty pounds upward forms one of the fine game fishes of the ocean. It comes in great schools and is taken trolling. To enjoy it fully a rowboat is preferred, or a boat that can be stopped quickly.

The tackle should be a tarpon or tuna rod of

nine or sixteen ounces, as the angler may wish; but the nine-ounce rod, No. 9 line, is heavy enough for rowboat fishing. In trolling from a big sailboat in the Nassau fashion, a big rod and No. 24 line is desirable.

In appearance the kingfish looks the part; long, lithe, powerful, iron-gray in color; and when leaping at the bait, which, as a rule, it does and *not after it is hooked,* it is a splendid sight. The bait is mullet or any small silvery fish, or squid. I have taken them with a white rag. The first rush of a big kingfish or cero and its play in general is a revelation to the angler. The members of the Tarpon Club now take it off Aransas Pass, going out trolling beyond the jetties.

There is another great game fish and cousin of the kingfish found here, but more rarely. This is the peto, or *Acanthocybium solandri,* found off the south of Key West and Tortugas in the Gulf Stream. It is a rare and splendid fish, occasionally caught when fishing for kingfish, running up to six feet in length and tipping the scales at one hundred or more pounds. The angler may go out for it, but the catch will be an accident, in my opinion, as in several years daily fishing on the Tortugas reef I saw very few.

Spanish Mackerel

Other large kingfish-like fishes are the escolaro of the *Lepidopidae* family. There are several genera and a number of species. It is taken off Key West and is common at Cuba where "escolaring" is a recognized sport. When it is known that escolars attain a weight of one hundred pounds it will be seen that here is a game fish to be conjured with.

Very similar to the kingfish in general appearance is the Spanish mackerel, *S. maculatus,* which may be termed a pigmy cero or kingfish; yet one of the finest of game fishes on very light tackle. It is an attractive mackerel-like fish, trim, debonair, beautifully marked with silver, blue above, with orange spots on its sides. It comes from the south in vast schools, and has been taken as far north as Cape Cod; but its real home is off Florida, on both sides of the Gulf of Mexico, where it is taken in great numbers. It rarely attains a weight of over twenty-five pounds, and the average fish is from four to six pounds. In 1909 I fished for Spanish mackerel in Aransas Pass, in water perfectly smooth. Scores of men and women were taking them with big bamboo rods and a short cotton line, small hook and shrimp bait. When a fish struck it was uncermoniously jerked into the emperian. I used an eight-ounce ten-foot split bamboo, a delicate silk line, and while I caught about one to ten of my neighbors I fancied I had more sport as the little four and six pounders made a splendid play on my light tackle, small hook and shrimp bait.

This was still fishing, as I allowed my boat to drift; but in Florida as at Biscayne Bay and about Miami the fish are usually taken trolling. Anglers bring in many at Long Key Camp. In trolling a jig or squid is used.

There is a Spanish mackerel, *S. sierra*, on the Pacific Coast, which I have taken at Santa Catalina though not in great numbers. Also the Monterey Spanish mackerel, *S. concolor*, taken trolling in the bay of Monterey, also in the San Clemente channel and off to the south of Santa Catalina, in September and October. The common mackerel when it can be taken, if captured with an eight-ounce trout rod or a stiff black bass rod, is a great game fish and when excited or biting it will take any kind of bait, a red rag or a silver spoon serving as well as bait. No trout of three pounds will make the sustained fight of a mackerel of the same weight, its rapid movements, its erratic play, long dashes about the boat on the resilient rod being a revelation to the angler who has the good fortune to try them on a fly rod.

Leaping Tuna

CHAPTER VII

THE PACIFIC COAST GROUNDS

GROUP 12

THE LEAPING TUNA

LEAVING the Gulf of Mexico region the sea angler may reach Southern California in two and one-half days, crossing Texas, an empire in itself, New Mexico and Arizona on the Sunset route from San Antonio to Los Angeles. Here is the Southern California sea angling ground including the islands of Santa Catalina, San Clemente, the Coronados, the Santa Barbara channel islands; all in all, the most remarkable sea angling region in the world. By this I do not mean that the angler can go out here and every day make a killing of leaping tuna. In this respect it is like other localities, fisherman's luck governs it; but here is a wonderful assortment of game fishes of large size, and best of all, a summer season, as a rule, devoid of squalls or storms of any kind from May to November, a fishing-ground that is semitropical, yet always cool and delightful. Most important, the island of Santa Catalina is so situated that it forms a vast lee or smooth water twenty or more miles out in the ocean. This is why it is so difficult to make tuna fishing a popular sport off New Jersey, Madeira, Block Island or Nova Scotia. The tuna is there and can be caught, but it is an oceanic fish, and to take it with any degree of comfort and safety there must be smooth water.

This is the secret of tuna fishing at Santa Catalina. Here, out at sea, in deep water, is water as smooth as a lake. As these lines are written, I have just watched and timed a friend playing a tuna for three hours and a half, in water twenty miles at sea, yet perfectly smooth.

Santa Catalina is an island sixty miles around, twenty-two long and from a quarter of a mile to eight miles wide. It is a big mountain range rising out of the ocean, with a marvelously cool summer climate and a winter that is the time of flowers, a cooler summer. On Avalon Bay is the town of Avalon, a town given over to angling, with all the appearance of a fashionable resort, hotels, cottages, etc., with three or four sea-going steamers per day in the season and one in winter, and from six to eight thousand inhabitants.

The interesting features of this town to the visiting angler are the boatmen's pier and the Tuna Club. The former is a long pier reaching out into the water, lined on both sides with the stands of boatmen, each designated by name, and with a seat, a tackle box and photographs of their world-wide patrons with their catches. In the bay are scores of launches, built here to meet the exact situation, and the result is that we find sea angling reduced to the last word of comfort. The Santa Catalina angler does not put on his old clothes and make himself entirely miserable; he can go out in white flannel if he desires, and come back immaculate; all of which is understood by a glance at the launches and the methods of angling. Most of the boats are eighteen or twenty-foot gasoline launches, wide beam and high rail, so they are very steady. The eight- or ten-horse power engine is placed amidships, and the engineer, boatman and gaffer sits on the starboard side at the wheel and can put his right hand on the wheel, the left on the clutch, and stop the engine at once when the angler has a strike. The latter sits in the stern, and facing it, in which are two comfortable chairs. One angler fishes to the right, one to the left.

The boats are equipped with the finest and most expensive tackle—six-ounce rods and six-thread lines, nine-ounce rods and nine-thread lines for fish up to sixty pounds, and sixteen-ounce rods and number twenty-one lines for tuna and swordfish. They also have kites for imitating the flight of the flyingfish, sleds for deflecting the bait one or two hundred feet away from the boat, gaffs, harpoons; in fact a complete equipment which is provided for $10 per day for one, two or three persons though only two can fish at a time. Half a day's angling is generally all that is desired, or from 7 A. M. to 12 M. This makes the expense $5 or $6 for two anglers or $3 a piece for boat, gaffer, bait, tackle, etc.

The boatman provides everything, the finest tackle, the only condition being that if the angler uses the expensive rods and lines of the boatman he must replace them if broken or lost.

In imagination we may assume that a boatman has been secured and we are going out for the elusive tuna. The boatman has obtained a number of flying fishes, about eighteen inches long. The launch rounds up at the private dock of the Tuna Club and we step aboard. The rod is sixteen ounces in weight, seven or seven and a half feet in length. The line is No. 24, with a seven-foot piano-wire leader and a No. 10 O'Shaughnessy hook. Reaching the outer water the line is paid out one hundred feet or so, the rod resting on the knee. The boat moves along slowly or fast, as the boatman may think necessary; but the main impression is of comfort, cleanliness, safety, and enjoyment in the fine views of the mountainous island, the calm, still deep-blue water; and here we may leave the anglers to glance at the tuna.

The tuna, tunny, horse mackerel, it is all one, is a fish of world-wide distribution, especially common in the Mediterranean Sea and in Southern Californian waters. It is a great mackerel-like fish, attaining a weight of one thousand or more pounds and a length of eleven feet. For some reason the average fish in the Mediterranean Sea, where are famous fisheries over a century old, is 175 pounds. On the Massachusetts coast, north of Cape Cod and to the mouth of the St. Lawrence, fishes run up to 800 or 1400 pounds. Ten miles off the New Jersey coast, in rough water or water liable to be rough, and off Block Island, the average is 60 or 70 pounds, and at Santa Catalina the average tuna (*Thunnus thynnus*) is 150 pounds.

This peculiarity and the positive assurance of smooth water has made Santa Catalina Island famous for its tuna angling; as a 150-pound fish is about the limit of angling *enjoyment* with rod and reel. When the fish runs up to 250 or 300 pounds it becomes labor and entails dangerous exertion. I took my first large tuna at this island in 1889, the fish that caused the founding of the Tuna Club. The fish towed me and a heavy boat about twelve miles in three hours, and I fought it without resting, using only a thumb pad of leather as a brake.

The tunas spawn along this island and formerly came in every July, and remained two months, affording great sport; but the Italian and Greek market fishermen, with the Japanese, by persistently netting this shore-line and spawning-ground, succeeded in practically driving these fishes away and ruining one of the greatest sporting assets America ever had.

It is interesting to note how Dr. Henry Van Dyke regarded this. He wrote the following after a day's fishing with the author:

"The efforts of the Tuna Club to secure protection for the great game fishes of the

Pacific coast, are worthy of the support of every patriotic Californian. Let the process of grabbing these fishes with nets on their spawning beds among the islands be continued for a few years longer, and one of the big assets of the state will be absolutely destroyed. And for what? To increase the profits of a few private corporations dealing in fish.

When these fishes have been exterminated, they can never be replaced. The occupation of the poor fishermen will be gone, a valuable source of food supply will be cut off, one of the attractions which draws visitors from all parts of the world to California will be lost forever.

No state is rich enough to allow such a waste of the property of all the people for the temporary advantage of a few.

The legislature will render a real public service by forbidding the capture of the great game fishes at such seasons and in such places and ways as seem to threaten the species with extinction. All honest men, whether they are anglers or not, would approve and commend this action of California in defending one of her magnificient natural resources."

The author and the Tuna Club fought for years for some legal protection to this coast, that Dr. Jordan has pronounced a spawning-bed, with no result. The politicians were afraid of the market fishermen's vote, but in 1913 an unusually intelligent lot of men were elected to the legislature. I made a report to the great Fish and Game Convention of the State of California on the conditions at Santa Catalina and San Clemente, and the threatened extinction of the great game and market fishes.

Mr. E. L. Hedderly, editor of *Western Field,* drew a bill setting aside the spawning-beds three miles offshore as a fish refuge and prohibiting all market netting. It was no less than a miracle, looking back at the twenty years of endeavor; but the legislature passed the bill and Governor Johnson promptly signed it. This righteous bill went into effect August 12, 1913, and for the first time in fifteen years the north coast of Santa Catalina for thirty-three miles was not netted day and night with long gill-nets running out into the ocean at intervals of every quarter of a mile, more or less.

On about the 15th of August a large school of tunas came up from the south, and *not* running into the miles of deadly nets, they remained near shore. On September 16th there was the first good tuna fishing at Santa Catalina Island in fifteen years, and it is believed that there will be a great increase in all the game fishes. A more notable illustration of reckless destruction of a great fishery and its saving at the eleventh hour was never known.

The leaping tuna in normal years comes in June or July and remains until September 15 or October 1. The vast schools lie off the island in deep water, but near the surface, and periodically raid the flying fishes, driving them into the bays and out onto the sands. At such times scores of schools can be seen on the surface and approached, and the bait cast at them with success. But the usual angling method is to troll with one hundred or one hundred and fifty feet of line astern, with a 21- or 24-line, a piano-wire leader, eight or nine feet long, broken by several swivels, and a No. 10, or No. 12 hook, baited with a pound and a quarter flying fish.

We will assume that one of our anglers has a strike. Two big tunas have come up astern with a rush. One takes the bait and is off, the click singing. The angler holds his tip up, endeavoring to apply brake or drag, the boatman stopping the launch and throwing her back. Between the knees of the angler, fastened to the seat, is a leather butt cap into which he has fitted the butt, and with this as a fulcrum he is ready to play the game.

The reel deserves attention, as it is large enough to hold six or eight hundred feet of a No. 21 line, wet; as perfect as a clock, and costing from $50 to $100 if it is a real tuna reel by the best maker. The first few moments the fine reel does the work with its brakes and sings; but if the fish is over one hundred and fifty pounds the angler should stop it before it takes five hundred feet of line; when this happens he begins to reel, and from then on it depends on the angler. The landing has been done in twenty minutes and in fourteen hours, but the man who lands a tuna of over one hundred pounds in less than forty minutes has performed heroic work.

There is a great difference in fishes, but the fish of one hundred and fifty to two hundred pounds, in its *best* condition, is a match for the best man with rod and reel. When the fish is brought to the surface the boatman brings out his gaff with an eight-foot handle, fastened to a rope, gaffs the fish under the head and holds it, and the deed is done. Volumes could be filled with the exciting adventures of the seventy or more anglers who have taken a one-hundred-pound leaping tuna, thus qualifying for membership in the Tuna Club.

The tuna spawns in the waters near shore; the young go into deeper water and do not return until they are of adult growth. This tuna does not leave the water after it is hooked, except on very rare occasions. It is called leaping tuna on account of its wonderful leaps after flying fish when feeding.

The first very large tuna was taken by the writer in 1889 with a sixteen-ounce rod and twenty-one-thread line. It weighed 183 pounds. This record was beaten the following year by the late Col. C. P. Morehous with a 251-pounder, which has stood ever since, though Mr. Ross of Montreal took off Canada a 600-pounder, but with a larger line and not under the rules which hold in the Tuna Club. The angler who defeats the Tuna Club record will take many prizes. It is estimated that $150,000 has been expended by anglers in a vain attempt to break it.

Various efforts have been made by the Tuna Club members to find satisfactory tuna fishing elsewhere. Mr. Aflalo investigated the Madeira Islands, but it was too rough. Mr. Earlscliffe attempted it in the Mediterranean, but Santa Catalina is the only place where the natural conditions are such as to make this sport a real pleasure. Even at San Clemente Island, where the tunas go, and San Nicolas, the sea is too rough and there is no lee. Playing a heavy fish in a seaway, where the waves are the greatest danger to the line and where one is liable to be caught in a squall ten miles out to sea, may be exciting, but it is not adapted to the long play often required in the case of a 150- or 200-pound tuna. Some of the tuna records of the Tuna Club, made in the tournaments, are as follows:

RECORDS

Angler	Date	Weight
Chas. F. Holder	1898	183 pounds
C. P. Morehous, Pasadena	1899	251 "
A. W. Barrett, Los Angeles	1900	164 "
Mrs. E. N. Dickinson, New York	1902	216 "
E. E. Ford, Alhambra	1902	174 "
John E. Stearns, Los Angeles	1902	197 "
A. W. Barrett, Los Angeles	1904	131 "
Phil. S. O'Mara, Salt Lake	1909	153 "
L. G. Murphy, Indiana	1910	175¼ "
C. B. Stocton, Los Angeles	1911	170 "

No tunas under one hundred pounds are counted, and when it is announced that no tunas have been taken, it means that no fish over one hundred pounds in weight has been taken with rod and reel.

Brief mention of the Tuna Club may not be out of place at this juncture. The club was founded by the author in 1889, to form a gentlemen's club that should take an interest in the conservation of game fishes, fresh and salt, in all California. The club has a commodious clubhouse, which it owns, on Avalon Bay. It gives two tournaments yearly; has several thousand dollars' worth of beautiful prizes, and performs a valuable work in aiding in saving the fisheries and elevating the sport standards all over the country. It has three hundred or more members and enrolls on its list some of the most distinguished anglers and sportsmen in the world. Among them are Lord Desborough, W. D. Coggeshall, Senator George F. Edmunds, Charles Hallock, Admiral Peary, Winston Churchill, Dan C. Beard, Dr. George E. Hale, David Starr Jordan, Gifford Pinchot, Prince d'Arenberg, Gen. John W. Foster, J. K. L. Ross, Dr. Henry Van Dyke, Colonel Roosevelt, Stewart Edward White, Caspar Whitney, and many more famed as anglers or for services in the interests of the conservation of the fisheries.

The club's spring tournament is a notable event in the field of sea angling, and every game fish of the region—white sea bass, tuna, black sea bass, yellowtail, swordfish, etc.—has a prize or many prizes in the different classes, all with the object of inducing the angler to fish with the lightest tackle and give the game fair play. The result? Fifteen years ago boats would go out with six or eight big hand-lines and come in with half a ton of splendid fish, running up to thirty pounds, which were dumped into the bay. To-day each of the possible one hundred angling launches of Avalon is equipped with the finest rods, reels, and lines. Such a thing as a hand-line is unknown. All of the thousands of anglers fish with dainty rods and lines, and a splendid standard of sport prevails. The Tuna Club cups and trophies are on exhibition, and its living room or hall has one of the most interesting exhibits of oceanic fishes to be found in the world, all the records of the members.

Group 13

THE YELLOW-FIN TUNA

THE second tuna in point of sporting value as a game fish at Santa Catalina and San Clemente, California, is the yellow-fin tuna, *Thunnus maculata*. Hang up the three species side by side and this fish will appear to be a cross between the leaping tuna and the long-fin tuna; but it is a fish of pronounced individuality. It associates with the long-fin tuna, but I have never seen it in schools of the leaping tuna. It is a beautiful fish, with green back, silver belly, and lemon-yellow finlets; the eye large and lustrous; a beautiful fish in the water, dignified, and graceful, with all the cleverness of a trout.

For years the yellow-fin tuna has been known in Japan and Honolulu, but it was not recognized as a Santa Catalina fish until 1890, when vast schools appeared, and it at once took its place as a game fish of the first quality. Driven away by the netters, described in a previous chapter, it deserted the island for years, but at the present writing is back again and filling the waters of the Santa Catalina lee and channel with life.

So thick were these fish at San Clemente in 1913 that they almost ruined the sport with the swordfish. Mr. Hooper of the Tuna Club, Vice-President of the Winchester Arms Company, told me that he could not get his swordfish bait overboard without hooking a tuna. In a trip within a few days tunas were hooked by a companion off Avalon Bay, and I saw men in skiffs playing them.

The yellow-fin tuna ranges up to four feet in length and one hundred pounds in weight, but the average fish is fifty pounds and the rod record sixty pounds. The school of 1913 averaged forty pounds. This fish is taken on a nine-ounce rod and a No. 9 line with a breaking strength of eighteen pounds; that is, the line will lift a dead weight of eighteen pounds. They have also been taken on the 3-6 tackle. The bait is a large sardine or smelt.

Not long ago when we were moving along at a rate of four or five miles an hour, the strike came, and my companion hooked a tuna. It was eight o'clock, and he landed the fish at about eleven, or three hours later, during which time the fish towed the boat at least two miles. It repeatedly came to surface. This fish was foul hooked, and I quote it to show the strength and staying power of the fish, so characteristic of the family.

While this tuna will bite readily on sardines, I have spent a day endeavoring to lure one. We were drifting and when the boatman tossed over a handful of bait they would rush at it, but carefully avoid the baited hook I dropped. This tuna feeds on small fishes, occasionally flying fish, and in September goes down deep and gorges itself on squid, schools of which are found here in deep water. It spawns near shore along Santa Catalina in August and September and disappears in October, probably going to some deep outer bank "where the siren sings," or it may go down the Mexican coast to warmer waters. Some of the records of the Tuna Club are:

Angler	Date	Weight
Arthur J. Eddy, Chicago..........	1906	60 pounds
E. J. Polkinhorn, Pasadena.......	1907	50½ "
F. T. Newport, Arcadia, Cal.......	1911	54 "

Group 14

THE LONG-FIN TUNA

THIS fish, *Thunnus alalonga,* has a wide range over the world, there being but one species and one genera. It is the smallest of all tunas, the average weight being but twenty-five pounds. I have been told by reliable fishermen that they had seen one-hundred-pounders. The fish is shorter, plumper than the others; its back a rich blue, its belly silver; the eyes large and hypnotic. It has the little finlets, numbering eight, which in the leaping tuna number nine, and in the yellow-fin tuna nine, but they are blue or dark instead of lemon-yellow.

It is essentially a tuna with the exception of the side fins, which are of extraordinary size, reaching from the first spine of the dorsal to the anal fin, or almost half the length of the body, and the most noticeable feature. If we trim off these fins we have a very good imitation of a leaping tuna or yellow-fin; in a word, the resemblance is strong. In its habits

Long-fin Tuna

this tuna differs greatly from the others. It is almost non-migratory here and normally can be found in great numbers at any time from a mile to two miles off Avalon Bay, rarely if ever going any nearer and ranging the blue waters to a depth of several hundred feet, but normally lying near the surface.

It is the fish the anglers all rely upon at Santa Catalina when everything else is out of season; it can almost always be caught if the season is not particularly stormy; then it disappears for a month or so. It feeds on small fishes and will bite so readily that it is often a nuisance. But it makes a violent and vicious play, plunging down into the deeps and often wearing out the lusty angler. It should be taken with a nine-ounce rod, nine-thread line, No. 10 or No. 12 hook, and sardine or smelt bait. The piano-wire leader here need not be over a foot or six inches long. A small sinker is generally attached to take the line down below the surface a foot or so; indeed, such a sinker is used for all these fishes, so that bait will not lie above the surface when trolling.

This tuna spawns along the kelp beds of Santa Catalina, now a fish refuge by the act of legislature secured by the Tuna Club in 1913. The eggs are deposited in August and September, but the very young are rarely seen here, the smallest fish being a five- or six-pounder, showing that they keep in deep water, out of sight.

All these tunas are of importance. In the Mediterranean the tunny fighters are of great value and the young tuna of fifty pounds, as served at the banquets of the Tuna Club, is meaty and rich. The yellow-fin is also a food fish, and the long-fin tuna is the one that is canned as "Blue Sea Tuna" and now constitutes the supply of a great business. While this tuna should be taken with a nine-ounce rod, it can be caught with 3-6 tackle. In using this, the angler should wear a belt with a rod socket and he can stand and play the game. In all this fishing there is what is termed "pumping." In water a mile deep, fish when hooked go down, instead of leaping as they do in the shallows, and when a long-fin tuna is stopped at the three-hundred-foot mark he must be lifted up, a proceeding to which he objects strenuously.

If you could see him now! He is pointed downward, head down, tail up, boring down. To offset or overcome this—sulking, it is termed in salmon angling—the angler holds his rod steady, reels the tip down to the surface, checks the line with one of his left-hand fingers (on the rod), and lifts the fish steadily until the rod is vertical or at an angle of sixty degrees; then the rod is dropped to the water suddenly, the angler reeling rapidly, and before the fish realizes it he has gained several feet. This is repeated, and is known as "pumping," as the angler makes an up-and-down movement. This is at first difficult, but it soon becomes automatic; the lift with the left hand, the sudden change of the right from the lower grip to the reel handle, etc., and when once understood is easily done and the fish brought to the surface. But if the latter is foul-hooked it may be a matter of hours. The long-fin tuna cups and trophies of the Tuna Club are many —cups, medals, medallions, etc. The club records with rod and reel are interesting and are as follows:

Angler	Date		Weight
Chas. W. Miller, Denver...	1901		30 pounds
Ernest Fallon, Los Angeles	1902		35 "
John Van Liew, " "	1903		38 "
Stewart Ingraham "	1904		46 "
J. W. McIntyre, Illinois....	1908	(winter)	65¼ "
W. N. McMillan, Nairobi, Africa	1910		50 "
Frank Kelly, Indiana.......	1911-12	(winter)	66¼ "
Frank B. Hoyt, Oakland...	1913	(winter)	50 "

Most of these tunas were taken on nine-ounce rods and No. 9 lines, with a breaking strength of eighteen pounds. Thus, if the angler in his excitement in playing a fifty-pounder puts on a greater strain than eighteen pounds, the line snaps.

Group 15

THE LITTLE TUNNIES

THE Bonitos of California so closely resemble the big tunas that it is evident they are close kinsmen. One, the oceanic bonito, is one of the fine game fishes in early spring in the Santa Catalina channel—the wide deep channel that lies between Santa Catalina Island and the mainland. Its specific name is *Gymnosarda pelamis.* It has a pronounced turn or dip in the lateral line below the second dorsal fin and four lengthwise stripes on its side below the lateral line, this distinguishing it from the Atlantic species.

It attains a length of two feet. I have taken specimens up to twenty pounds, and consider it one of the hard fighting fishes of the region. It roams the temperate seas in schools loosely connected, and spawns in the sheltered lee of Santa Catalina and San Clemente in June and July. So erratic is the appearance of this fish that its catch is very uncertain; hence anglers cannot depend or rely upon it. It is a fish to be taken on a six-ounce rod and given a chance for its life on a No. 6 line. The lure is a sardine or smelt or Wilson spoon, with moderate speed.

Associated nearly always with the long-fin tuna on the surface of the deep Santa Catalina channel is the California bonito, or skipjack; a plump, radiant little fish of the tunny tribe, known to science as *Sarda chilensis.* It ranges up and down the coast from Patagonia to San Francisco, and is particularly common at Santa Catalina. The best way to take it is to go out a mile or two in the lee of the island where the water is smooth, and have the boatman toss over chum or ground fish until the bonitos come to the surface. They are so tame that they come about the boat and almost take the bait from the hand. Now the angler can bait his hook with a sardine, cast at the bonito he wishes, and take him. The vigor of the little fish is extraordinary. I once watched a young lady play one over an hour before she could land it. This bonito turned out to be a record fish, a twenty-pounder. It played, as do most of the bonitos, entirely on the surface, making great circles and rushes.

No fish is more beautiful than this marine humming-bird as it comes in. Its back is a deep blue; its belly silver, and over all is an investment of old rose-pink, and it scintillates in the sun like a prism. It has a very different movement from other fishes. The body is very plump and thick-set, and in swimming the tail apparently is wriggled violently, the side fins used very little. In the long-fin tuna the extraordinary long pectoral or side fins, more than half the length of the fish, are not used, in all probability, to swim with, but are balancers; I have seen them held two or three inches from the body while the fish was driving itself along by its tail.

The bonito is a common article of food, and a game fish to be conjured with on light tackle. The average catch does not weigh over six or seven pounds. The Tuna Club record for the bonito is twenty pounds.

Group 16

THE BLACK SEA BASS

NO one can angle long in Southern Californian waters without being startled when reeling in a line by the apparition of an enormous black or gray fish dashing to the surface after the bait, causing the water to swirl and foam as, perchance, it misses it and goes back to the bottom.

This might be a shark, but it is the black sea bass, *Stereolepis gigas,* a gigantic member of the bass family and not to be confused with the Florida jewfish, being a totally different fish. The black sea bass appears to be born big, at least I have never seen one under one hundred pounds, but I have heard of a fifty-pounder and know a man who said he had seen one of two pounds. But as for very little black sea bass no one, apparently, has ever seen one, although the fish spawns in the kelp beds of the islands in August and September. They come in from the outer deeps in May and June, and in July, August, and September

Black Sea Bass

are in full possession of the kelp beds, aquatic forests, and can almost always be taken back of Avalon in a great kelp forest in water thirty or fifty feet deep.

I have taken an eighty-pounder with a nine-ounce rod, but the big ones (and in the Gulf of California they attain a weight of one thousand pounds—reported) require tuna tackle. The fish displays remarkable strength, especially when hard fought. If handled gently they can be manipulated easier. I have had many a bout with the black sea bass and more than once was outgeneraled.

The method of taking the fish is to go to the locality and use half a barracuda or six pounds of long-fin tuna for bait. This is lowered to within five feet of the bottom. The boat is buoyed to the anchor so that it can be cast off. Sooner or later the strike comes. The tuna comes at its lure like a bolt of lightning, but this giant nibbles at the bait, I have seen him do it. He hovers over it, passes it, turns about, all ready to become alarmed and rush away. I have watched him do all this sometimes standing on his head in the wonderful kelpian forest, an amazing and startling spectacle.

So, bearing this habit in mind, you are not

disturbed when the click of your reel begins to sound in the most deliberate fashion. You wait five or ten minutes, or until the line is running out with some regularity; then you give ten or twenty feet of line, according to the temperament of your boatman; then when it comes taut you strike and—the fight is on.

The game is a two-hundred-pounder, anyway, and possibly a three- or four-hundred-pound fish. The Tuna Club record is 436 pounds, by Mr. L. G. Murphy of Converse, Ind., in the season of 1905. In 1912 Mr. S. W. Guthrie of Los Angeles took a 427-pounder. The first rush is irresistible and two or three hundred feet of line may be taken before you can stop the fish; then it swims steadily on, towing a launch or rowboat, and making for the ocean forest, which, if it enters, the game is up.

So you fight, pull, and reel with judgment, never putting over forty-two pounds pressure on your line. In half an hour, or an hour, if you have luck, the leviathan is on the surface, a big, splendid replica of a fresh-water black bass, or as near that as anything. Your man gaffs him and with a block and tackle he is lifted on deck or fastened and towed in.

The black sea bass has all the habits of a

White Sea Bass

bass and is occasionally taken trolling, but the line should be provided with a sinker so that it will reach to within ten feet of the bottom. In trolling a five-pound whitefish or a flying fish is a good lure, and to see three hundred pounds of fish running up at your bait as you pull it rapidly in, is a revelation. The black sea bass appears in schools at times; is full of spawn in August and September, and disappears practically from its summer resorts in November, though certain fishes can be taken in certain localities at almost any time.

Some of the Tuna Club rod records are as follows:

Angler	Date	Weight
S. W. Guthrie, Los Angeles.......	1912	427 pounds
J. S. Dempsey, Kentucky..........	1911	430 "
Jesse Roberts, Philadelphia........	1910	385 "
R. S. Baird, San Francisco........	1909	394 "
C. J. Tripp, Los Angeles..........	1907	427 "

Group 17

THE WHITE SEA BASS

IN traveling around the world the angler will find old friends but slightly changed in different lands. Thus, the South Africander has his kabeljou, a great fish which is the weakfish in New York. Crossing the continent he finds a species in the Gulf of California weighing one hundred pounds. At Santa Catalina he catches a fish called the white sea bass, *Cynoscion nobilis,* a near cousin. The Californian fish averages thirty pounds and runs up to eighty; is a fine game fish, arriving in April and May at Santa Catalina in vast schools and providing sport of the best quality. It spawns along the island kelp beds in July, and late in the summer and fall is taken in numbers farther north, as in Monterey Bay.

The white sea bass is a long, grayish, silvery fish, looking much like a salmon, five or six feet in length, and when a school dashes into Avalon Bay after sardines it is a spectacle to be remembered. When not feeding, the bass lies in broken schools in the great kelp beds, poising like birds among the branches.

The tackle used is a nine-ounce rod, nine-thread line, short leader of piano-wire, and No. 12 hook. Live bait, mackerel or sardine, is the most effective. The boat is allowed to drift, but the greater number of fish are taken trolling with a flying fish or a Wilson spoon. I have taken five fifty-pounders in one day in Avalon Bay with live bait. Their play on the surface adds to the conclusion that they have few superiors as a great game fish.

The rod record of the Tuna Club is a sixty-pounder, taken by Mr. C. H. Harding of Philadelphia. In playing this fish the angler should wear the leather belt with a butt socket and stand and play the fish comfortably.

The so-called sea-trout of Southern Californian waters is but another species, and another is found further north, while the giant of Mexico, which I have taken at Guaymas and at Tobari, one hundred miles south, is *C. macdonaldi,* all having the same general habit and all are game fishes in the best sense. The smaller ones are well adapted to the trout rod of eight ounces.

At Santa Catalina the white sea bass is an early spring fish, though it sometimes remains into September, and can be found along the islands of Santa Catalina and San Clemente in water from twenty to thirty feet in depth, or in harbors like San Luis Obispo, where there is no surf, also at Redondo.

Yellowtail

Group 18

THE YELLOWTAIL

THE amber-jack of the Pacific coast is the yellowtail, *Seriola dorsalis.* It is literally the fish of the people, or to Southern Californians what the bluefish is to the New Englanders. It has a wide range, from Mexico to Monterey Bay, but its normal home, where it is always to be found from April to December, is the shores of the Santa Catalina channel islands of California, especially San Clemente, famous for its thirty- and forty-pound yellowtails, that can be caught at times as fast as the line is dropped over. Again the yellowtail will flaunt its charms of blue, old-gold, and silver in your face, five feet from the boat, yet scorn the bait that hides the hook, thus proving itself the cleverest of the game fishes of the sea.

I think the judgment of all sea anglers is that the yellowtail, " pound for pound," as Dr. Henshall has it, is the hardest fighting of all the game fishes of the sea. The fish of twenty-seven or thirty pounds, or even seventeen or twenty pounds, never discovers that he is beaten, he never acknowledges it, and the tyro only conquers one on fair tackle after a long struggle.

A volume could be written on the yellowtail and the tricks it plays on verdant anglers; how it has pulled men and boys overboard; how it bites ravenously to-day and scorns the lure to-morrow. On the Pacific coast, if the winter is mild, with little rain, it will remain at the islands all the year, and I have caught it nearly every week in the year at Avalon. But its custom is to leave in December, going out to some deep offshore plateau, where it remains until March or April, when it begins to move inshore, doubtless following the vast schools of sardines, anchovies, or smelts.

There are several definite "runs" at Santa Catalina or San Clemente recognized by the fishermen; one early in April, another in June, but they are uncertain. Some years the yellowtails will come in vast numbers, so that in my experience it was impossible to lower a bait without hooking a twenty- or thirty-pound fish. The following year yellowtail angling would draw a blank. One year they are at San Clemente, and very few at Santa Catalina; the next year they are at Redondo, on the mainland, in numbers; but, as a rule, they are found in great numbers at the islands off the city of Los Angeles.

The fish attains a length of five feet and a weight of eighty pounds, but the average catch is a twenty-five pounder, and the rod record is sixty and one-half pounds, held by Mr. W. W. Simpson, a member of the Tuna Club, of Winkley, Whalley, England. This fish is in the British Museum, with a replica of the rod, reel, and line used by Mr. Simpson in taking it, at San Clemente, off Los Angeles County, California.

The yellowtail is one of the most beautiful of all fishes; a deep green above, with a yellow median line, tail and fins often a vivid lemon-yellow; the belly pure silver; the eye large and brilliant, the head large; the fish looking for all the world like a giant bluefish, but with a long, fine dorsal fin and powerful tail. It is very erratic in its movements; now in schools, now living a solitary life; in winter often coming up on hooks set in eight hundred feet of water; now basking in the sun, swimming slowly in schools on the surface or dashing like furies into bays, chasing the small fry out onto the beach. It is essentially a deep-water fish;

that is, it is not found on shores where there is a surf, but on the surface of the deep channels and in summer it, doubtless, rarely goes below one hundred feet.

The fish is more or less carnivorous, feeding on sardines, anchovies, flying fish, or squid. It is found to spawn in August and September, but very small fishes are never seen, and doubtless take to deep waters or some secluded place. The tackle for big yellowtail is the nine-ounce rod and No. 9 line with No. 10 hook, a foot of piano-wire leader, and as bait a flying fish. If smaller fish are desired, the 3-6 tackle should be used with sardine bait, trolling slowly not far from shore along the kelp. It is well to toss over chum, and, to my mind, the ideal yellowtail angling is had by allowing the bait to drift, attracting the fish to it by tossing over bait, then casting with the 3-6 tackle and hooking them in plain sight. Such a locality is Ship Rock, Santa Catalina. In 1912, with Dr. Gifford Pinchot, we took thirteen or fourteen big fellows in a forenoon, experimenting with various tackle, the fish biting the moment the sardine sank out of sight.

The cups, medals, etc., for yellowtail at the Tuna Club are many, and in the tournaments it is the favorite catch, due to its pugnacity and hard fighting qualities. When yellowtails are scarce alongshore anglers hunt for them at sea beneath beds of floating kelp. Here they often strike the beautiful dolphin, that changes its colors as it comes in, yellow-green and gold, a marvelous sight. The fish plays so like the yellowtail that the angler does not know the difference until it is brought to gaff. In this way the rare rooster-fish, *Papagalo nematistius,* is sometimes taken, which I have hooked at Guaymas, where it is a common fish.

Group 19

SMALL GAME FISHES OF THE PACIFIC COAST

A VOLUME could be written on the small game fishes alone of the Santa Catalina Channel islands. The whitefish, up to ten pounds, is a vigorous game always to be counted on from early spring to late fall, in rather deep water; sardine bait and nine-ounce rod. Nearer shore we find that sheepshead, a big-headed fish of ten or fifteen pounds, with black and red alternating stripes in the adult, the female all gray, white, or red. This fish makes a game play and is fond of abalone and crayfish bait, but will not scorn sardine. At San Clemente, in the shallows, they can be caught in great numbers.

In the kelp beds are countless rock bass of several species that range up to four or five pounds. At San Nicolas Island I have taken ten-pound rock bass, of a dark-green hue, that made a valiant play. In schools about the rocks and in the kelp beds is the blue-eyed perch, a fish of from one to four pounds, with

Yellow-fin Tuna

Whitefish

Mackerel

a small mouth, gray tints, and beautiful blue eyes. It is rarely caught, as the angler uses too large a hook and does not bait for it with abalone, crab, or crayfish, which it loves. Another little fish, blue, with stripes, is the blacksmith, that makes a savage fight, while the striped perch of two pounds and the splendid sand-bass of eight or ten pounds are occasionally taken, to demonstrate to the angler that in the variety, as well as game qualities, of its fishes California stands well to the fore.

Outside of the kelp we may see schools of the California mackerel, and myriads of barracudas from six to twelve pounds. In the little bays, like Silver Cañon, on sandy bottom, lie fine California halibut, which will rise to the surface and take a sardine, and go rippling away, making a splendid play. Here, too, are several rays that are game; a leaping oil-shark, that is an understudy to the tarpon, while the big hammerhead and bonito-sharks afford sport for the strenuous. Singularly enough, anglers are rarely troubled with sharks here as in Florida.

At Silver Cañon, Santa Catalina, just outside the surf, are found the roncador (*Umbrina*), the yellow-fin (*Seriphus politus*), the surf-fish (*Menticirrus undulatus*)—all game fishes requiring crab, crayfish, or clam bait, as it is their custom to lie in the surf, or just beyond it, and hunt for the little sand-crabs washed out by the waves. The gulls prey on them from the shore side, while the roncadors lie in wait in the undertow.

In the deeper waters the sea-trout, a small white sea bass, is found with large smelts and a variety of small fry too numerous to mention—all of which, and those mentioned in this chapter should be angled for with a light rod of six ounces and No. 6 line and hook adapted to the fish. Thus, rock bass will take a large No. 10 or No. 12 hook; but the blue-eyed perch requires a very small hook, a No. 8 or 12 fly-hook size, and the same is true of the blacksmith and the Medialuna.

In San Francisco Bay the tom cod is a game fish, and the striped bass is game to conjure with by trolling along the flats with a Wilson spoon or bait—crayfish, crab, or abalone. About the Santa Barbara channel islands practically the same fishes are taken, but the islands stand end-on to the prevailing inshore wind; hence there is little or no smooth water to be counted on, though the mornings are often smooth; but the west wind and frequent fog comes rolling in, and the angler here should be sure of his boat and boatman and take no chances. All the channel islands are twenty or more miles at sea and the angler should always go in a boat with an experienced boatman, except at Santa Catalina, where the bays of Avalon and Cabrillo are always smooth and perfectly safe. The San Clemente channel, between that island and Santa Catalina, is rough in the afternoon, so boatmen making the passage leave at four o'clock in the morning, making the trip on smooth seas, the wind not rising until ten o'clock or so.

Group 20

THE SHORE FISHES OF THE PACIFIC

THE region from Cape Mendocino to the Mexican line at Coronado on the Pacific coast abounds in towns where every facility is provided for the angler. Some of these are Santa Monica, Santa Barbara, Redondo, Venice, Hermosa Beach, Seal Beach, Huntington Beach, Long Beach, San Pedro, Portugese Bend, Bay City, Alamitos, Laguna, Newport, Del Mar, Ocean Side, Coronado, Bay City, and others, all nearly all on long sandy beaches where the great sea fishes described do not come in, as they do not like surf or the sandy water. Only one of these beaches, Redondo, occasionally has the yellowtail and other fishing, from the pier or beach, and this is due to the fact that a deep channel cuts in at Redondo. If, then, you wish yellowtail, bonito, and the tunas at these towns, you must take the local market boats, or a launch, and go out due west of the shore into the channel for from one mile to five, where by trolling the fishes may be had. Black sea bass may be found in the kelp beds and at the entrance to San Diego harbor.

All these beach towns are devoted to other fishing, and nearly all have long piers which reach out over the surf and are patronized by anglers from far and near, who use long, stiff bamboo rods, clam and fish bait, and catch a variety of small fishes—mackerel, smelt, croakers, surf, sharks, rays, sculpins, halibut, and others. The long California beaches afford a field for the angler similar to those of the Atlantic angler on the Jersey coast. Here the members of the Los Angeles Rod and Reel Club display their skill and have reduced the sport of beach angling to a science. You may see their long rods thrust into the sand almost anywhere from Santa Barbara to La Jolla or the Mexican line. The game fish is the surf, or California whiting, *Menticirrhus undulatus,* a fine game fish at four or five pounds. Here also is the yellow-fin *Seriphus politus,* the spot-fin croaker, *Roncador stearnsi.* There is also a little roncador or croaker, *Genyonemis lineatus.*

The yellow-fin, *Seriphus politus,* is one of the most beautiful of all the surf-fishes; tinted gold, silver, and yellow, and adapting itself in a marvelous fashion to the color of the bottom. This fish is also to be had all alongshore and in numbers at Silver Cañon, Santa Catalina, where it lies in deeper water off the beach where at times a heavy surf rolls in. The tyro might fish here or anywhere alongshore for these fishes and not suspect their presence, simply by not using the right kind of bait. Yellowtail, halibut, whitefish, and others are taken here with sardine bait, but surf-fish never, or hardly ever. Clam, crayfish, or abalone bait is used for them, principally the first mentioned, when a good catch will be made—and good sport be enjoyed. When angling for surf-fish with a six-ounce rod, a halibut is often a possibility, and specimens weighing sixty pounds have been taken.

Perhaps the most interesting fish caught on the mainland shores is the ladyfish, *Albula vulpes;* I have seen specimens two feet in length at Santa Monica. Possibly the best locality for them is in Anaheim Bay, Alamitos Bay, and at Newport Bay, where they find the smooth, shallow waters suited to their taste and habit. When hooked, the ladyfish acts in a very unladylike manner, leaping in a frenzy and dancing around, calling to mind the gyrations of a maddened tarpon.

The golden croaker, *Umbrina roncador;* the yellow-fin, *Seriphus politus;* the spot-fin croaker, *Roncador stearnsi;* the California surf whiting, *Menticirrhus undulatus,* form a group of most interesting fishes, and in Southern California have literally thousands of devotees. Special trains are run on the railroads to the beaches to accommodate the anglers, and the fine piers and beaches form the field for the "try-outs" in the great summer and winter tournaments of the Los Angeles Rod and Reel Club, of which Mr. Charles V. Barton of Los Angeles is secretary and Mr. Max Loewenthal president. The club offers handsome prizes for the various events.

This great fishing ground of Southern California is so situated that strange fishes come across from the west and up from the south, giving it a remarkable fish fauna; hence the angler is liable at any time to take strange fishes, as the dolphin, the bottle-nose dolphin (a whale), taken by Col. John E. Stearns; the fine game fish, pomfret, *Bramaraii;* the so-called pompano, *Peritus simillium,* the opha, and Luvarus jack. All these fishes can be seen in the rooms of the Tuna Club.

The angling piers of California are unique. At Redondo you find a little shop at the entrance with long rods and tackle to rent, and not far away the bait man, ready to provide clams, small fish, or anything you wish. Long Beach has several piers, and at Venice the pier is virtually a city street built out over the sea, with shops of various kinds and entertainments sufficient to divert the attention of the ghost of Walton. At the long, mile or more, pier at Santa Monica a house stands at the sea-end, far out to sea, and the rail is lined with anglers who employ strange tackle. A little shop provides simple cheer to the physical man, and tackle can be rented and bait purchased. Back of the shop hangs a big scoop-net forty feet square, which is occasionally lowered and live bait caught, which is sold to the anglers whose ambition soars above sand-dabs and mackerel to the other realms of yellowtail or big sharks, or a possible ray.

GROUP 21

STRIPED BASS IN CALIFORNIA

ANGLERS who enjoy the inspiriting New Jersey coast will find the same fish sport of the striped bass angling about San Francisco, into the waters of which it was introduced some years ago. Now the splendid fish is thoroughly acclimated and is the best market and game fish of the region.

The bass follow small fry onto the San Pablo and other flats in the bay and are found in the river and sloughs where they can be taken at the last half of the ebb and first half of the flood tide. They are generally caught by trolling with a Wilson spoon from a small boat. The visitor who knows nothing of the conditions will waste time without a good boatman, as the angling is peculiar and it is necessary to know among other things that a brass spoon is the thing when the water is clear and an all silver one when it is thick, and while lobster appeals to the cuttyhunk Puritan bass, clam is the *bonne bouche* in the San Francisco sloughs. San

Antonio and Wingo sloughs are the best. A fifty-five-pounder has been taken here. The best time is from August 1st to December, November and December possibly being the best months for large fish. In East Oakland and San Leandro estuaries the striped bass is found in April on until late fall. At San Pablo and Rodeo the best time is March, April and May. The 9-ounce rod or 3-6 tackle is adequate for this game was a 6/0 hook and an assortment of Wilson spoons—No. 4, No. 5 or No. 6/0.

Group 22

THE SEA SALMON

THERE are countless salmon on the Pacific coast and a number of varieties which appeal to the angler; but the chief among ten thousand is the king salmon or chinook, *Oncorphynchus tschawytscha.* This fish, like the rest, will not take a fly except very rarely though I have heard that it will at Vancouver. The Atlantic salmon, *Salmo salar,* is not found here, but the chinook spends the winter offshore near the mouth of the Sacramento, Rogue, Klamath, and Columbia rivers, and in the late summer can be found from Monterey or Del Monte to Vancouver and beyond, everywhere affording excellent fishing with bait or spoon.

In August the great schools of chinook can be found in Monterey Bay, five or six miles from Capitola or Santa Cruz, and near Del Monte or Monterey, there being a salmon cannery at the latter city about one hundred miles south of San Francisco. The angler will find the best of accommodations at Del Monte, Capitola or Santa Cruz in large and commodious hotels or boarding houses. If these localities had proper boats, light but safe, seagoing launches on the Santa Catalina plan, anglers would have a better chance, but as it is, mostly nondescript fishing boats are used, and really enjoyable rod fishing is to be had only by the angler who goes out in a rowboat towed by some big launch, which can be had at Santa Cruz or Del Monte.

The salmon appear to be lying about forty feet deep, feeding on the large schools of anchovies found here, and are fat and in fine condition for the long swim they are soon to take. When the school is located by your boatman, with a hand-line and a heavy sinker, baited with a sardine, you may begin fishing with a rod. I used my 9-ounce yellowtail rod with No. 9 line and a No. 12 hook baited with a large sardine. It was necessary to get the sardine down to the fish, so a heavy sinker was employed, an ominous move so far as any pleasure with a rod is concerned, as what fish could play with a heavy flat sinker dangling about his head? I avoided this by by using an appliance invented by Mr. Parker

J. Whitney, a veteran angler for salmon here. I doubled my line into a loop about a foot long, tied a piece of common thread on to one side, ran this through a pipe sinker and attached it to the opposite side of the loop. The object will be evident. When a salmon strikes the bait the slightest jerk breaks the thread, the pipe sinker drops off, and the angler has the salmon to play free of the leaden encumbrance. I tried this successfully and had excellent sport with salmon and white sea bass.

In angling here there is always a large fleet of nondescript craft ranging from the professional market boats of the Japanese to the angler who is endeavoring to take his game in a sportsmanlike manner.

These salmon run up to eighty pounds, but a forty-pounder is a good average. The boats go out at six o'clock, or soon after sunrise, from Del Monte, Capitola or Santa Cruz and by nine or ten the sport should be on. The water should be smooth though there may be a ground swell in the great open bay. Suddenly, by eleven o'clock, earlier or later, a rushing sound is heard and looking seaward the angler sees a wall of foam coming on. This is caused by the so-called "trade" wind that rises daily all alongshore. This in a short time raises a sea and the majority of the boats set sail for home, though the market men continue to troll for salmon in the fine stiff breeze with its rising sea.

All along up the coast these fishes can be taken; now with sardine, now with a Wilson spoon. With the latter I have taken them on the Williamson River, a branch of Klamath Lake, Oregon. Eureka, California, affords, at the mouth of the Eel River, some of the finest sea angling in the state—salmon, cod and other game; and this may be found all alongshore to the north—Oregon, Washington, Vancouver, to Alaska.

The time for salmon in Monterey is June, July and August, varying with seasons. In August the San Francisco anglers find them at Potato Patch and Duxbury Reef, an hour from the ferry, or Sausalito, opposite San Francisco, or Tiburon where boats can be had. San Francisco anglers use a large hook and fresh sardine bait, also No. 7 Wilson spoon, with a torpedo sinker and a long-handle-gaff. Having located a school of sardines troll (drag the bait slowly). In August the chinooks enter San Francisco bay on their way up the Sacramento and San Joaquin rivers at which time they can be had at near Lime Point and Rancoon Straits by trolling with a No. 6 or No. 7 Wilson spoon (copper and silver).

The salt water salmon fishing may be said to begin in May and end September 15th. Launches can be secured at Santa Cruz at $7.50 per half day for the salmon fishing in Monterey Bay or at Monterey or Del Monte.

While the steelhead is a rainbow trout and this volume treats only of sea fishes, mention should be made of the big steelheads as they are caught in the ocean in winter and spring. One of the best localities is Eureka, and another is the salt water laguna at the mouth of the Santa Inez River near the town of Lompoc, Santa Barbara Co., Cal. Here in April the finest sport has been had either trolling from boats with a spoon or casting from the bank. The fall run after the first rain, when the water breaks through from the laguna to the sea is productive of good sport. An 8-ounce rod, E line and spoon is the lure. The Russian and other rivers around San Francisco are famous regions for this game fish.

Group 23

THE SANTA CATALINA ISLAND SWORDFISH

WHILE two swordfishes are found in California, the *Xiphias* or flat-bill is an exceptional catch, the *Tetrapturus* or common Santa Catalina swordfish a very common one. The members of the Tuna Club of Avalon Bay took one hundred with rod and reel in 1912, and a greater number in 1913.

The *Xiphias* is bulky, heavier and more compact than the latter; its sword is longer and flatter, and the fish is more of a living ram or dreadnaught. Individuals ranging up to one thousand pounds have been seen and an eight-hundred-pounder was caught in a net at Santa Catalina in 1902.

The Santa Catalina Island swordfish, on the other hand, is lighter, longer, more trim and slender. The sword is more like a rapier than a sabre, and is shorter than in *Xiphias*. The fish has fifteen stripes, white on a blue ground, and is a more graceful fish than the fighter so common off Block Island and such a well known market fish in Massachusetts. This swordfish comes in from somewhere in August, sometimes in July, often in vast schools covering a square mile in the San Clemente channel. Then they break up and are seen in pairs, either swimming along with the big fins out of water, or lying prone on the surface seemingly asleep. The fish are doubtless spawning; they affect the lee of the islands and are seen feeding near shore, taking the rock bass, fiying fish and others.

By September, the warmest month in California, though always cool on the water, they will take a bait, and scores of anglers are now out after them. Many fish at Santa Catalina Island; others take a large launch and go to San Clemente. The charge is $15 per day for such a boat, which holds five or six comfortably. As the Shade camp is established at the island, anglers can live ashore. San Clemente is a governmental island, leased to Mr. Chas. Howland as a sheep ranch, and permission must be obtained before camping or landing. This courtesy should be observed. No one is refused if the proprieties are observed.

Seated in the comfortable launch, previously described, the anglers unreel their 21-strand lines to a length of one hundred and fifty feet or so. You will observe that this wonderful line, that breaks at a strain of forty-two pounds, has red, blue and green silk wound about it at intervals, so when the angler sees red silk going over he knows one hundred feet is gone; green one hundred and fifty, and so on. The line has previously been wet to avoid friction. The rod is a 16-ounce affair, one long tip and short butt; the reel holds six hundred or more feet of line, and is a wonderful machine with drags and click, which can be set at any tension, and when a swordfish strikes all the angler has to do is to hold on to the handle as the line cannot break if the reel is set properly. The reel is on top of the rod, and the angler's left hand, if he is fishing on the left, or port side, grasps the upper grip, his right the lower grip on the butt. The rod rests over his knee and at an angle of forty-five degrees, to deflect his bait away from that of his companion at his side on the starboard side. If the baits meet confusion worse confounded results. The line has a piano-wire leader of fine steel eight or ten feet long, with several brass swivels. The hook is the best No. 10, to be had, and the ancient O'Shaughnessy type is mostly used, though there are many others doubtless equally as effective. A sinker is attached to keep the bait down. The latter is a flying fish.

Once out a half-mile or so, your boatman, who is also gaffer, engineer and general adviser, suggests the " kite," a novel idea suggested by Capt. George Farnsworth, of Avalon, a noted big fish gaffer. You notice that he has an ordinary square kite which he puts up by sending the launch ahead rapidly, then he reeves the line through a ring attached to the kite. The boatman holds the kite cord, the angler his rod, and the launch is now moving along at about five miles an hour, towing the kite which is sixty or so feet in air, the angler's line leading to it through the ring and away to the bait in the water. The flying fish makes long leaps when alarmed, and, sustained by its wing-like fins, covers an eighth of a mile. The splash of the return of the flying fish to the water excites the predatory fishes and by jerking on his line and using the kite as a fulcrum, the boatman can successfully imitate this jump. Often the game is seen, its big dorsal and the tip of the caudal fin appearing high above the surface. We will assume that it is now seen by our anglers. The bait is jerked into the air, falls with a splash in front of the big fish; there is a swirl of water and the bait is taken.

The mouth of the swordfish is toothless and of hard gristle, so it is necessary to give the fish time. In a word, do not strike on the instant, as with trout; wait a few seconds, then taking up the slack with a few turns of the reel handle the angler gives the game the butt. His companion has of course reeled in his line to avoid complications. The boatman has stopped the launch and she floats on the perfectly ideal and smooth water under the shadow of the island mountains, on lake-like water, yet twenty miles out at sea from the mainland.

The moment the swordfish feels the hook it is liable to make a terrific rush; then goes up into the air and standing virtually on its tail, dashes away in any direction. These leaps are extraordinary manifestations, and while I have never observed more than ten or twelve leaps of a tarpon on my rod, this swordfish will make fifty or more, and to see a fish ten feet in length going off, or coming at you standing on its tail, is a sight for the gods. At times, held by the line, it will circle the boat; again go into the air shake itself wildly, to fall with a crash. There appears to be no limit to its posturing in air, and it is not imaginary as I have photographs taken by Capt. George Michaelis and others, which show the fish in air. Dr. Gifford Pinchot counted fifty leaps of a swordfish before he brought it to gaff. I was following him in the launch and I fancied I could hear the return of the big fish as I was directly behind them. It was pitch dark and a heavy sea running in the San Clemente channel, so I did not see the fish leap; but I have seen a *Tetrapturus* go an estimated ten feet into the air and drop with a crash, after the manner of the ray.

An expert angler with good wind can outplay a large *Tetrapturus* in from twenty minutes to one hour if the fish is not over two or three hundred pounds. If it is a very large fish it is likely to take more time.

At last the game is brought near the boat and is going about it sullenly in great circles. It is the same fish that has rammed many a ship and forced the men to the pumps, and there is every chance of its ramming the boat and sending her to the bottom. Mr. Joseph Reed of Pasadena told me of a similar instance off Block Island, when a harpooned Xiphias came at the dory and sent its sword through it. This has never happened at Santa Catalina or San Clemente.

The game within reach, the boatman grasps his long-handled gaff that has a long rope attached to the handle. Nearer comes the fish, and as it is reeled into this particular sphere of action the gaffer drops the steel point and hooks onto the swordfish in the under jaw, lifts its head quickly out of water and holds it while it strikes vicious blows with head or tail. This is the moment of supreme triumph for the weary angler. He stands and watches the exciting dénouement, soaked in the flurry, and rejoices like a "strong man." And well he may, as the splendid fish is perhaps eleven feet in length and weighs anywhere from two hundred and fifty to three hundred and fifty pounds. It is a beautiful creature in the sunlight; a pure intense blue, with fifteen light-gray vertical stripes, giving it a tiger-like appearance. It has a long rapier-like sword, a domed forehead, large hypnotic staring eyes, powerful tail, which is now beating the water and tossing it over the men. But this is the end; the fish is soon killed, and hauled aboard and the blue flag of the Tuna Club goes to the top and they turn in to the Tuna Club, or to the pier at Avalon or Cabrillo, to have the official weigher take it, who also photographs it for the records of the club.

Another appliance used is called the "sled." This is a little floating sled which is attached to the line above the bait and headed away from the launch, and as she moves the sled carries the bait one hundred or more feet away from her. In the case of a timid fish this is a deadly scheme as the game is not alarmed by the launch.

This new sport—swordfish angling with rod and reel—is in a class by itself and, all in all, when the danger, the leaps and the spectacular play is considered, I should place it ahead of leaping tuna or tarpon. The leaping tuna is unquestionably the hardest fighting fish known to anglers; I mean by this, the tuna in its best condition, and when the angler fights his fish standing off fairly and forcing the fish to come to him, instead of rushing the launch at the tuna and gaffing him before he knows where he is. In this way tunas have been taken in ten minutes, but the anglers who introduced tuna fishing—Doran, Macomber, Morehous, and others in 1889-90-91 had 16-ounce rods, No. 21 lines and big reels with no drag but a leather pad which was pressed on the line with the thumb of the right hand.

The fight was made in a rowboat, and the boatman always had instructions to pull away from the fish while the angler fought him; the idea being to give the fish a square deal. This explains the long plays of Wood and Elms, fourteen hours; Beaman, ten hours; my own fish, four hours; Morehous, four hours (the record fish). The angler fought the fish to a finish, and so intense and exhausting were some of these contests that several fatalities have occurred. The African buffalo and rhinoceros are believed to be two of the most dangerous and difficult animals to capture, but I recall one night when some members of the Tuna Club just over from Africa were comparing the sports—landing a two or three hundred-pound leaping tuna at its best, and killing a rhinoceros—arguing as to which was the most difficult feat, the palm was given to the doughty tuna.

The swordfish has not the strength of the tuna, but it is a spectacular fish. Its leaps and dashes on its tail are extraordinary manifestations of rage and astonishment, and when it can be taken in smooth waters, in a region where the climate is perfect in its relation to comfort it will be agreed that the new game is worthy its first place among the game fishes of the sea. The rod and reel record for this fish, on file at the Tuna Club, are as follows:

Angler	Date	Weight
W. C. Boschen, New York.........	1913	355 pounds
C. G. Conn. Elkhart..............	1909	339 "
Col. John E. Stearns, Los Angeles	1910	292 "
L. G. Murphy, Converse, Ind.......	1912	318 "
Edward Llewellyn, Los Angeles...	1903	125 "
Jesse Roberts, Philadelphia........	1911	282 "
Geo. E. Pillsbury, Jr., Los Angeles	1908	138 "
F. T. Newport, Arcadia, Cal.......	1912	214 "

APPENDIX

AN ANGLING ITINERARY

THE fishes described in this volume can all be taken in an arranged itinerary, and supposing the reader to be a sea angler the following general plan can be followed; not personally conducted, rather go as you please. While the plan includes only sea angling the traveling angler can fill in the links with incursions into the ranks of trout or black bass in whatever locality he may be.

We may start from New York in spring; try the bay fishing, then to the coast of New Jersey for surf fishing, the striped bass at Harvey Cedars, the train to the gulf coast of Florida for tarpon. A few days on the Indian River, and down the coast to Long Key Camp or to Key West. Then across the Gulf by steamer or cars to New Orleans and on to San Antonio, trying the tarpon at Port Aransas, the headquarters of the Tarpon Club, Mr. Cotter, secretary. A week or two here with tarpon, jewfish, kingfish and channel bass, and the angler crosses Texas, Arizona, and New Mexico to California and Santa Catalina and San Clemente islands, where tuna, yellowtail, white sea bass, swordfish and others await, according to time and season.

From here he moves on to Del Monte, Capitola or Santa Cruz and tries the chinook salmon in Monterey Bay, then the striped bass in San Francisco Bay. He then goes to Eureka by boat or cars for the salmon and sea-trout fishing in the mouth of the Eel River, from there, perhaps, to Klamath for rainbow trout, and on to Vancouver for more salmon. From this point the angler may be tempted to go to Alaska or to the Yellowstone for trout and to Montana or Idaho and back East by the Canadian Pacific and its lakes, arriving at the St. Lawrence for the fall fishing; then down through Maine to the Rangeley and other lakes for trout, bass and land-locked salmon, coming again to New York having completed the most remarkable angling trip in the world.

BIBLIOGRAPHY

As the present volume is intended as only suggestive of the sea fishing of America the following books may aid the reader in obtaining greater detail relating to the great sea game fishes:

The Book of the Tuna Club Avalon, Cal.

American Food and Game Fishes (Jordan), Doubleday & Page, New York.

The Book of the Tarpon (Dimock), Outing Publishing Co., New York.

The Game Fishes of the World (Holder), Geo. W. Doran Co., New York.

The Channel Islands of California (Hol der), A. C. McClurg & Co., Chicago.

The East Florida Fishes and How to Catch Them (W. H. Gregg).

The Game Books of the Southern Pacific Co. (James Horsburgh, Jr.), Flood Building, San Francisco, Cal.

Game Fishes of California, Dodge Pub. Co., New York.

Angler's Guide, Field and Stream Co., New York.

Fishing Kits and Equipment (Samuel G. Camp) Outing Publishing Co., New York.

American Fishes (Goode), Estes & Lauriat, Boston.

Fish Stories (Dr. David Starr Jordan), Henry Holt & Co., New York.

Big game at Sea (Holder), Outing Publishing Co., New York.

The Log of a Sea Angler (Holder) Houghton, Mifflin & Co., Boston.

Angling Map of Southern California, A. T. Santa Fé R. R., Los Angeles, Cal.

ANGLING CLUBS

The secretaries of the following clubs are willing to provide information as to the angling: The Asbury Park, N. J., Fishing Club. The Tarpon Club of Texas, Port Aransas. The Tarpon Club of Tampico, Mexico, Mr. Poindexter. The Tuna Club, Avalon, Santa Catalina Island, Cal. The California Rod and Reel Club, Los Angeles, Max Loewenthal, Pres. The Striped Bass Club, San Francisco. The Galveston Rod and Reel Club, Galveston,

The San Francisco Fly Casting Club. The Angling Club of New York. The Tarpon Club, St. Petersburg, Florida.

CLIMATE

What kind of climate the angler may expect in the various angling fiields herein described will be of interest. The Florida winters are delightful, and from December to April the angler will find fishing of some description and conditions similar to those in the north in summer. The climate at Key West is particularly delightful. When the time for tarpon arrives in April or May, possibly March, it rapidly becomes warmer and more or less humidity may be expected, but it is pleasant on the water. The author has spent several seasons, winter and summer, on the outer reef beyond Key West, and it is hot, yet the enthusiastic angler will not mind it and a trip to the Florida reef in summer is worth while. The heat is tropical and it is moist—all metal rusts and clothing moulds, and the government has not yet eradicated the mosquito. In fishing at Garden Key I wore the minimum attire and went overboard several times a day. I went to Aransas Pass, Texas, for tarpon in August and found it a very comfortable region for a semitropic one. A peculiar southeast wind blows nearly every summer day on the island, and I never found it disagreeably hot on the water; nor did I mind it ashore. Of course it is hot, and the angler needs thin clothing and little of it.

California

In entering the regions recommended for sea angling on the Pacific coast the angler finds an entirely different state of affairs. Thus in leaving Florida or Texas or any eastern state from Massachusetts to the Mexican line in August and going to the California coast, particularly the islands offshore he finds a very different climate. Here the heat is dry, lacking in humidity, and on the Santa Catalina, San Clemente, Coronada or Santa Barbara grounds offshore the angler finds an almost perfect climate, cool and delightful, really uncomfortably warm days being the exception. The government Weather Bureau has a branch station at the Tuna Club, and the club makes the reports, showing the climate of Avalon Bay to be well nigh perfect the year around; frost very rare and really hot days in summer the exception. I can compare it only to Maine, and in

May, June, July, August, September, and October, day after day is perfect, cool, and delightful on the water, with the mercury averaging as follows:

January, February, March (in the shade), 63°. Temperature of the ocean, 64°. General average in August, 67° (shade). Highest average summer temperature, 72°; the lowest, 65°. Highest in August, 74° (in the shade). Highest in September, on one day, 81°. The lowest temperature ever recorded in December in Avalon was 51°; the highest, 64°. The lowest sea bathing temperature for December was 58°; the highest, 64°.

If I were to mention a possible fault with the California climate I should say that the nights are too cool; so cool, indeed, that there is very little night boating, as in the East. This being so, anglers dress in California as they do in the East, the Florida equipment of linen and white duck being too thin, out of place, and rarely seen. This holds for the entire Pacific coast in summer.

Equipment

The habitual sea angler of course owns his rods and has a tackle bag equipped with all the paraphernalia required in out-of-the-way places. But the occasional angler, who has not such possessions will often find himself without tackle, and in the heart of good fishing. Before taking a trip to such fishing grounds a call should be made at some first class tackle shop in London or New York, as Mills, Abbey and Imbrie, Edwin Vom Hofe, New York, Hardy or Farlow, London, and there are others. It is economy to buy the best of everything. It is difficult to get good tackle in Nassau and in many places in Florida. In Aransas Pass, Texas, tackle may be rented. At Long Key Camp it can be either rented or purchased. In California there are good outfitting shops, as Tuft-Lyons or B. H. Dyas Company in Los Angeles, and several in San Franscico and Portland, Ore. At Santa Catalina Island, at the town of Avalon, there are two tackle outfiitting establishments where the best New York and Los Angeles tackle, rods and reels can be had. More than this, every boatman here includes the use of the best tackle in the rent of the boat, which is $10 per day or $6 per half day, the understanding being that the angler replaces the tackle injured, lost or broken—a not unreasonable rule when rods, reels and lines are the best made and naturally expensive.

Angling Grounds

New York

Around New York, the Sound, Great South Bay and the lower bay are more or less secluded waters. To go outside to the deep sea banks the angler takes one of the numerous steamers that are in the business in summer.

Florida

From New York to Florida alongshore there is a succession of sandy low beaches on which the sea pounds. I doubt if there is a rock or stone or a real hill in all the distance; hence all the angling is off the beach or in some inlet, or in the mouth of rivers, as the St. Mary or St. John's. Coming to Florida we find a great outside island or stretch of sand inclosing a long body of water with runs out into the Gulf Stream and back again through various passes. This island lake is called Indian River. The lagoons begin in latitude 29°, or thereabouts, at or near New Smyrna in Mosquito Lagoon and continue to Jupiter, latitude 27°, or thereabouts

All along this coast there is fine angling and equipped with W. H. Gregg's "Where, When, How to Catch Fish on the East Coast of Florida," a voluminous, conscientious, and perfectly reliable book on Florida fishing, the angler cannot fail to find the best of sport.

Florida Reef

The trip to Florida and to Key West by rail alone, aside from the fishing is an experience every sea angler should have. The Florida Keys and the reef begin in a general way at Jupiter on the east coast. Here you are in Biscayne Bay and have fine fishing at Fowey Rocks, and down the coast, inside and out; in fact, as I have previously said, anywhere in a radius of two hundred miles from Cape Sable north or south there is fine fishing. At Long Key Camp we find the famous angling or fishing camp in the heart of the wonderful keys which end in the Tortugas group, where I spent a number of years, winter and summer, fishing for the wonderful fishes, over six hundred of which, from pompano to tarpon, are game on the right tackle. From Key West, sixty miles west, the Tortugas group can be reached. At Loggerhead Key the Carnegie Institute maintains a biological station.

California

Los Angeles, a city of 600,000, is headquarters for anglers going to the channel islands and Los Angeles Port is but eighteen miles from the north end of Santa Catalina, where the little town of Cabrillo affords the finest fishing on the island. It is beautifully located on an isthmus and directly opposite is a land-locked harbor where, it is said, Cabrillo wintered when he discovered the island in 1542 and, one hundred years later, Vizcaino.

Santa Catalina is the only island that has a town and regular lines of steamers. Avalon, the largest port, is a town of from 5,000 to 8,000 in summer; has hotels, boarding houses, camps, shops, fleets of boats, and is a thoroughly wide awake town, situated on Avalon Bay thirty miles from Los Angeles. There are three steamers daily in summer and one in winter. The island is twenty-two miles long and about sixty around; a big mountain range rising from the sea. Of all the islands it lies northwest and southeast; its north side affording a perfect lee and protected coves, thus making the big game fish angling possible.

The Coronados to the south have good fishing, but are uninhabited, dry rocks in Mexican waters. The Santa Barbara Islands—Santa Rosa, Anacapa, Santa Cruz, and San Miguel—lie one hundred miles to the north of the Santa Catalina group. They are all private property and permission must be obtained to land. The fishing is good, but, due to their east and west position, the islands are subject to heavy winds and have no lee like that at Santa Catalina. To reach them boats may be chartered at Santa Catalina, San Pedro, or Santa Barbara. Large boats are necessary and the trip should not be made without an experienced skipper. Such a man is Captain Larco of Santa Barbara.

THE END

INDEX

www.ingramcontent.com/pod-product-compliance
Lightning Source LLC
LaVergne TN
LVHW010617100826
845148LV00014B/3011